★
ICONS

D1492940

C26410

Cover:
Jantzen Swim Suits, 1949
Endpapers:
Wurlitzer, 1947
Page 1:
Seagram's, 1945

© 2003 TASCHEN GmbH
Hohenzollernring 53, D–50672 Köln
www.taschen.com

Editor: Jim Heimann, Los Angeles
Layout: Claudia Frey, Cologne
Cover Design: Claudia Frey and Angelika Taschen, Cologne
Production: Tina Ciborowius, Cologne
Editorial coordination: Sonja Altmeppen, Cologne
German translation: Stefan Barmann, Cologne
French translation: Simone Manceau, Paris
Spanish translation: Gemma Deza Guil for LocTeam, S. L., Barcelona
Japanese translation: Mari Kiyomiya, Chiba

Printed in Italy
ISBN 3–8228–2399–6
ISBN 4–88783–193–5 (edition with Japanese cover)

ALL-AMERICAN ADS
40^S

Ed. Jim Heimann

TASCHEN

KÖLN LONDON LOS ANGELES MADRID PARIS TOKYO

The 1940s

From Rationing to Prosperity, American Life in the 1940s

by Willy R. Wilkerson III

In 1941 America was at war and a blackout was in effect after 6 p.m. from coast to coast. The year before, Oldsmobile had proclaimed it had produced the "Most Modern Car In The World." But now car manufacturers retooled in a matter of months to make tanks — 102,351 in all — and built a whopping 2,455,964 trucks for the Army by war's end. Women assembled bombers that their husbands and boyfriends would fly to the front lines.

Although many companies had switched to manufacturing products truly essential to the war effort, makers of inexpensive luxury goods declared that their products, too, were indispensable. Coca-Cola pronounced "I'm Loyal To Quality" while Chesterfield Cigarettes urged consumers on "From Here To Victory."

At the beginning of the war, American merchant ships were being sunk in record numbers off the East Coast by wolf packs of German U-boats. The War Department issued posters warning the public to guard against loose talk. Posters went up everywhere, including bus stations and in tram terminals – of a drawing of a ship sinking with the slogan underneath, "Loose Lips Sink Ships."

The military might of the U.S. would have foundered without the aid of War Bonds. To help promote the war effort, the film industry also went to war, retooling to produce propaganda films instead of features. Filmmakers like Frank Capra spearheaded the propaganda war with his series *Why We Fight*. Pathé newsreels that ran before films in movie theaters were the evening news of the 1940s. Movie stars traded makeup for uniforms to sell War Bonds or to join the ranks. USO tours, of which Bob Hope was the supreme master of ceremonies, brought much needed entertainment and a boost in morale to the troops.

At home, food and gas rationing did not stop people from going out and having a good time. Despite blackouts and the problem of navigating dark streets, it was a different story in the nightclubs and restaurants in America. Business was booming.

The world was ushered into the Atomic Age in August, 1945, when the Allies dropped the first nuclear bomb on Hiroshima. With the Japanese surrender effectively ending the war in the Pacific a month later, America's love affair with the car began in earnest. The resulting jubilation sent people into a frenzy of spending and driving. 21.4 million new cars were sold between 1946 and 1950. In 1949 production topped the five million mark for the first time. While 222,862 passenger cars were built in 1943, a staggering 2,148,699 were built in 1946 with General Motors selling the lion's share of 1,240,418.

By 1946, the automobile had become the symbol of American freedom and independence. This new-found expression of freedom found Americans motoring from coast to coast after the war. More luxurious travel, however, was provided by trains and ocean liners. For those who had a fear of flying nothing could compare to the elegance of *The Queen Elizabeth* that insured passengers would be ferried from New York to Portsmouth in style, or the Pullman car which rivaled the ocean liners in luxury. The Pennsylvania Railroad advertised "It's always

fair weather..." as their trains hurtled through the American wilderness.
The post-war American Dream had its origins in the GI Bill. For the first time, affordable housing was made available to returning war veterans; and we have William J. Levitt to thank for for the first prefabricated housing development — Levittown — which used production line techniques similar to those utilized by the auto industry. Thus began the postwar migration from the cities to the suburbs. And those suburbs were booming with babies.

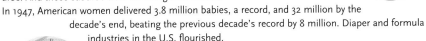

In 1947, American women delivered 3.8 million babies, a record, and 32 million by the decade's end, beating the previous decade's record by 8 million. Diaper and formula industries in the U.S. flourished.

In 1946, Hollywood returned to what it did best – making good movies. And there was no shortage. Within a year movies and radio were threatened by a new innovation every bit as revolutionary as sound was to silent movies in 1927: television. American families forsook their dining rooms and instead huddled in front of their Motorola or Zenith with their meals on their laps watching their favorite shows. Still, *Reader's Digest* continued to be the leading U.S. magazine, selling 9 million copies in 1949. *Life Magazine* ranked second, selling 5,305,394.

The advent of canned convenience food began during the war and was brought to American homes when the war ended. Boxed cereals like Kellogg's Corn Flakes asked "Has the war upset your breakfast habits?" Canned foods, now a staple of the American diet, saw their origins in *Spam*, the canned ham ration supplied to GIs during the war.

Alcohol and tobacco ads during the 1940s were the stuff of screen legends, of Humphrey Bogart smoking a Chesterfield and sipping Chivas Regal at Rick's place in *Casablanca*. Camel boldly advertised "More Doctors Smoke Camels", a statement that would definitely attract the attention of the Surgeon General today. Throughout the 1940s cigarette manufacturers sold a steady 300 million cigarettes a year, with aggregate sales of $357.3 million by decade's end.

Consumer products abounded after the war as companies again switched from manufacturing war equipment to consumer products. General Electric sold 100-watt light bulbs for fifteen cents a piece. Kodak film, which had captured the atrocities of war, now documented the pleasures of peacetime in summer backyard barbecues and Christmas gatherings. And for the home, no one could be without a refrigerator.

The end of the decade saw enormous economic prosperity in America spurred on by the wondrous advances in technology. But the end of one war only saw the beginning of another. The Cold War between Soviet Russia and the United States ignited the decades-long cat and mouse game between the two superpowers that became a reality when Russia acquired the A-Bomb. The fear of nuclear war was ever present, even in school classrooms. By the 1950s, children practiced air raid drills hiding under their desks and ordinary citizens dug bomb shelters in their backyards, making for an all-new kind of war effort on American soil.

Die Vierziger

Von der Rationierung zum Wohlstand: Der amerikanische Lebensstil in den Vierzigern

von Willy R. Wilkerson III

Man schrieb das Jahr 1941 und Amerika befand sich im Krieg. Nach sechs Uhr abends herrschte von Küste zu Küste Verdunkelung. Im Jahr zuvor hatte Oldsmobile verkündet, man habe das »Modernste Auto der Welt«. Doch jetzt rüsteten die Autohersteller innerhalb weniger Monate auf die Fabrikation von Panzern um, 102.351 insgesamt, und produzierten bis Kriegsende die horrende Zahl von 2.455.964 Lastwagen für die Armee.

In dieser Zeit der Umstellung behaupteten die Hersteller Genuss verheißender Artikel nur konsequent, auch ihre Produkte seien unverzichtbar. Coca Cola ließ erklären: »Ich bin loyal zur Qualität«, derweil Chesterfield die Verbraucher »Von hier aus zum Sieg« beorderte. Zu Beginn des Krieges wurden amerikanische Handelsschiffe in Rekordzahl und in Rudeltaktik von deutschen U-Booten versenkt. Deshalb warnte das Kriegsministerium die Öffentlichkeit vor unbedachten Äußerungen. Überall tauchten Plakate auf mit der Zeichnung eines untergehenden Schiffes und dem Slogan: »Loose Lips Sink Ships«.

Um die Kriegsanstrengungen voranzutreiben und für Kriegsanleihen zu werben, zog auch die Filmbranche zu Felde und rüstete von Spielfilmen auf Propagandastreifen um. Frank Capra zog mit seiner Serie *Why We Fight* als Erster in den Propagandakrieg. Die Pathé-Wochenschauen im Vorprogramm der Kinos waren so etwas wie die Sechs-Uhr-Nachrichten der Vierziger. Filmstars tauschten den Schminkkoffer gegen die Uniform. Und die Betreuungstouren der USO, deren oberster Zeremonienmeister Bob Hope war, brachten den Truppen die dringend benötigte Unterhaltung und moralische Unterstützung.

In der Heimat hielt die Rationierung von Lebensmitteln und Benzin die Menschen keineswegs davon ab, auszugehen und sich zu amüsieren. Trotz Verdunkelung und der Schwierigkeit, sich auf finsteren Straßen zurechtzufinden, boomte in Amerikas Nachtclubs das Geschäft.

Mit dem Abwurf der ersten Atombombe im August 1945 brach für die Welt das Nuklearzeitalter an. Nach der Kapitulation Japans, mit der einen Monat später der Krieg im Pazifik zu Ende ging, kam Amerikas Liebe zum Auto erst richtig in Schwung. 21,4 Millionen Neuwagen wurden zwischen 1946 und 1950 verkauft. 1949 überstieg die Produktion erstmals die Fünf-Millionen-Marke. Während 1943 nur 222.862 PKWs gebaut wurden, waren es 1946 sagenhafte 2.148.699.

Um 1946 wurde das Auto zum Symbol amerikanischer Freiheit und Unabhängigkeit. Dieses neue Selbstverständnis führte dazu, dass die Amerikaner nun von Küste zu Küste sausten. Elegant reisen konnte man mit Zügen und Ozeankreuzern. Wer an Flugangst litt, entschied sich für die unvergleichliche Eleganz der *Queen Elizabeth*, die eine stilvolle Überfahrt von New York nach Portsmouth gewährleistete, oder aber für den *Pullman*-Waggon, der in Sachen Luxus mit den Ozeanriesen wetteiferte. Wovon nach Kriegsende ganz Amerika träumte – das G.I.-Gesetz machte es erstmals möglich: Heimkehrende Veteranen sollten sich ein Eigenheim leisten können. Dem New Yorker Geschäftsmann William J. Levitt war die erste Neubau-

siedlung aus Fertighäusern zu verdanken – Levittown. Die Idee war bei der serien-
mäßigen Produktion von Autos abgeguckt. Von nun an war die Abwanderung
aus den Innen- in die Vorstädte ebenso wenig aufzuhalten wie der Babyboom.
1947 brachten die amerikanischen Frauen 3,8 Millionen Babies zur Welt, und
zum Ende des Jahrzehnts verzeichnete man 32 Millionen Neugeborene, womit
der Rekord der dreißiger Jahre um 8 Millionen überboten wurde. Die Herstellung
von Windeln und Säuglingsnahrung war in den USA ein blühendes Geschäft.
Hollywood kehrt 1946 zurück zu dem, was es am besten konnte – gute Filme produzie-
ren. Und das nicht zu knapp. Allerdings drohte Film und Hörfunk ein Jahr später eine
Innovation, die in jeder Hinsicht so umwälzend wirkte wie 1927 der Ton für den
Stummfilm: das Fernsehen. Amerikanische Familien drängten sich mit dem Essen
auf dem Schoß vor ihrem Motorola- oder Zenith-Apparat und schauten sich ihre
Lieblingssendungen an. Unbeschadet von dieser Entwicklung blieb *Reader's
Digest* das führende Magazin der USA und verkaufte 1949 eine Auflage von 9
Millionen. An zweiter Stelle kam das *Life Magazine* mit 5.305.394 Exemplaren.
Nach Kriegsende hielten abgepackte Fertiggerichte Einzug in amerikanische
Küchen. Getreideflocken wie Kellogg's Corn Flakes warfen die Frage auf: »Hat der
Krieg ihre Frühstücksgewohnheiten ins Wanken gebracht?« Die Konservennahrung, nun ein Grundbe-
standteil auf dem Speisezettel der Amerikaner, ging zurück auf *Spam*, die Dosenration Pressschinken,
die die G.I.s im Krieg bekamen.
Alkohol- und Tabakwerbung war in den Vierzigern Stoff für Leinwandlegenden wie Humphrey Bogart –
in Rick's Café rauchte er Chesterfield und schlüfte Chivas Regal. Damals warb Camel ganz unverfroren:
»Mehr Ärzte rauchen Camel«, eine Aussage, die heute den Gesundheitsminister auf den Plan rufen
würde. In den Vierzigern setzten die Zigarettenhersteller jährlich 300 Millionen Zigaretten ab. Ihr
Umsatz belief sich gegen Ende des Jahrzehnts auf 357,3 Millionen Dollar.
Nach dem Krieg, als die Firmen wieder auf die Friedensproduktion umstellten, waren Konsumgüter
reichlich vorhanden. General Electric verkaufte 100-Watt-Birnen für 15 Cent das Stück. Kodak-Filme, die
die Gräuel des Krieges dokumentiert hatten, hielten nun bei Grillpartys und anderswo die Vergnügun-
gen der Friedenszeit fest.
Gegen Ende des Jahrzehnts erlebte Amerika einen ungeheuren wirtschaftlichen Aufschwung, der durch
wundersame Fortschritte der Technik vorangetrieben wurde. Doch das Ende des einen Krieges bedeu-
tete nur den Anfang des nächsten. Der Kalte Krieg zwischen der Sowjetunion und
den USA führte zu einem jahrzehntelangen Katz-und-Maus-Spiel zwischen den
beiden Supermächten. Aus Spiel wurde Ernst, als Russland in den Besitz der
Atombombe kam. Die Furcht vor einem nuklearen Krieg war allgegenwärtig.
Bald absolvierten selbst Kinder Luftangriffsübungen und verkrochen sich unter
ihren Schulpulten, während normale Bürger Luftschutzbunker in ihren Häu-
sern einrichteten und das Fundament für neue Kriegsanstrengungen auf ameri-
kanischem Boden legten.

Les Années 40

Du rationnement à la prospérité, la vie américaine dans les années 40

de Willy R. Wilkerson III

En 1941, l'Amérique est en guerre et après 18 heures, le black-out est en vigueur. L'année précédente, Oldsmobile a proposé « la voiture la plus moderne du monde », mais les constructeurs se sont reconvertis et produisent pour l'armée pas moins de 102 351 tanks et 2 455 964 camions. Les femmes fabriquent les bombardiers que leurs maris et petits amis pilotent jusqu'au front.

Mais entre les tanks et les avions de combat, d'autres industriels font savoir que leurs produits sont indispensables à l'effort de guerre. Coca-Cola affirme : « Je suis fidèle à la qualité », tandis que Chesterfield encourage ses consommateurs « d'ici jusqu'à la victoire. »

Au début de la guerre, d'innombrables navires marchands américains sont coulés au large de la côte est par des sous-marins allemands. Le Département de la guerre émet des affiches mettant en garde le public contre tout propos inconsidéré. On en voit partout, dans les gares routières, aux arrêts de tramway, avec un dessin de bateau qui coule et, en dessous, le slogan : « Les paroles s'égarent, les bateaux coulent. »

Sans le soutien des Emprunts de guerre, la puissance militaire américaine se serait effondrée. Pour favoriser l'effort de guerre, l'industrie du film est aussi partie au combat afin de produire des films de propagande. Des réalisateurs aussi réputés que Frank Capra ouvrent la voie avec des séries comme *Pourquoi nous combattons*, fer de lance de la propagande de guerre. Les actualités Pathé, projetées en salle avant les films, deviennent l'équivalent de notre journal de 20 heures. Les stars de l'écran troquent leur maquillage contre des uniformes. Elles vendent des titres d'emprunt ou s'enrôlent.

Au pays, le rationnement de nourriture et de gaz n'empêche pas les gens de sortir et de s'amuser. La vie continue dans les boîtes de nuit et les restaurants. Les affaires prospèrent.

En août 1945, le monde entre dans l'ère atomique, quand les Alliés lâchent la première bombe nucléaire sur Hiroshima. Un mois plus tard, avec la reddition japonaise qui met un point final à la guerre dans le Pacifique, l'histoire d'amour entre l'Amérique et la voiture peut enfin s'embraser. La jubilation qui s'en suit amène les gens non seulement à dépenser sans compter, mais aussi à conduire sans limite. Entre 1946 et 1950, 21,4 millions de voitures neuves sont vendues. En 1949, pour la première fois, la production atteint les cinq millions. Alors que 222 862 voitures de tourisme étaient construites en 1943, le chiffre époustouflant de 2 148 699 est atteint en 1946, et la General Motors s'octroie la part du lion avec 1 240 418 véhicules.

Dès 1946, l'automobile devient le symbole de la liberté et de l'indépendance. Ce nouveau mode d'expression permet de traverser le pays de l'Atlantique au Pacifique. Mais l'élégance reste attachée aux trains et aux paquebots. Pour ceux qui craignent de prendre l'avion, rien ne peut égaler le *Queen Elizabeth* qui assure aux passagers un confort maximum entre New York et Portsmouth, ni les wagons *Pullman* qui n'ont rien à envier aux navires de luxe.

Le rêve américain d'après-guerre repose sur les indemnités accordées aux G.I.'s.

Pour la première fois, les anciens combattants peuvent acquérir une demeure à un prix accessible. William J. Levitt construit le premier lotissement de maisons préfabriquées. Ainsi commence la migration d'après-guerre entre villes et banlieues.

En 1947, les femmes américaines ont donné naissance à 3,8 millions de bébés, un record. Il y en aura 32 millions à la fin de la décennie, soit 8 millions de plus que dans les années 30. L'industrie des couches et des petits pots connaît un boom.

En 1946, Hollywood revient à ce qu'elle fait de mieux : de bons films. Il y en aura à foison. Toutefois, films et radios sont menacés par une innovation aussi révolutionnaire que l'avait été le son pour les films muets. En effet, en 1947, la télévision envahit la salle de séjour des familles américaines. Celles-ci abandonnent leur salle à manger et vont s'entasser devant leur télé Motorola ou Zenith, un plateau repas sur les genoux, pour regarder leurs programmes préférés. Malgré tout, le *Reader's Digest* continue de s'affirmer comme le premier magazine américain et vend 9 millions de copies en 1949. *Life Magazine* vient en deuxième position avec 5 305 394 exemplaires. L'arrivée sur le marché des aliments en boîte débute pendant la guerre, puis se poursuit à l'intérieur des foyers. Les céréales comme Kellogg's Corn Flakes posent la question : « La guerre a-t-elle changé vos habitudes alimentaires ? » Les aliments en boîte, désormais produit de base, trouvent leur origine dans le Spam, ration de jambon en boîte fournie aux G. I.'s pendant la guerre.

Dans les années 40, les publicités pour l'alcool et le tabac étaient le domaine des grandes légendes de l'écran, telles Humphrey Bogart fumant des Chesterfield et dégustant un Chivas Regal chez Rick, à Casablanca. Camel n'hésitait pas à déclarer : « Tous les médecins fument des Camel », ce qui, aujourd'hui, ne manquerait pas d'alerter le Haut-Commissaire à la Santé.

Après la guerre, les produits abondent alors que les compagnies se reconvertissent dans la consommation. La General Electric vend les ampoules de 100 watts à quinze cents pièce. Les pellicules Kodak, témoins des atrocités en temps de guerre, enregistrent désormais les plaisirs du temps de paix, les barbecues d'été dans les jardins et les fêtes de Noël.

La fin de la décennie voit s'instaurer en Amérique une formidable prospérité économique s'appuyant sur d'extraordinaires progrès technologiques. Mais la fin d'une guerre entraîne le début d'une autre. Avec la guerre froide entre la Russie soviétique et les Etats-Unis commence entre les deux superpuissances une partie d'échecs qui va durer des décennies. Elle se concrétise quand la Russie se dote de la bombe atomique. La crainte d'une guerre nucléaire se retrouve dans les salles de classe des années 50 : les enfants pratiquent des exercices de raid aérien, se cachant sous leurs pupitres.

Los años cuarenta

Del racionamiento a la prosperidad, la vida en Estados Unidos en los años cuarenta

por Willy R. Wilkerson III

En 1941 Estados Unidos estaba en guerra y las luces debían permanecer apagadas a partir de las 18h de costa a costa. Oldsmobile, la marca que proclamaba haber creado «El automóvil más moderno del mundo», se dedicaba ahora, como el resto de fabricantes de automóviles, a la construcción de tanques (102.351 en total) y de camiones (2.455.964) para el ejército.

Muchas empresas modificaron su actividad para fabricar productos esenciales para la guerra. En cambio, los fabricantes de bienes de lujo más asequibles declaraban que sus productos también eran indispensables. Coca-Cola anunciaba: «Soy fiel a la calidad», y Chesterfield Cigarettes animaba a los consumidores con el lema: «De aquí a la victoria».

Al estallar la guerra, los submarinos alemanes apostados en la Costa Este hundieron numerosos barcos de mercancías estadounidenses. El Departamento de Guerra emitió carteles solicitando a la población la máxima discreción. Carteles en los que aparecía un barco naufragando sobre el eslogan: «Si los rumores se extienden, los barcos se hunden» invadieron las estaciones de autobuses y las terminales de tranvías.

La fuerza militar de Estados Unidos se habría ido a pique de no ser por los Bonos de Guerra. Para aliviar el gasto económico que suponía la guerra, la industria cinematográfica se dedicó a producir películas propagandísticas. Cineastas como Frank Capra hicieron propaganda a favor de la guerra con la serie documental *Why We Fight* (*Por qué luchamos*). Las estrellas de cine cambiaban el maquillaje por los uniformes para vender Bonos de Guerra o para alistarse a filas. Las giras USO, de las que Bob Hope fue el maestro supremo, alentaron a las tropas estadounidenses. En los hogares, el racionamiento de alimentos y gas no impidió que los estadounidenses salieran a la calle en busca de diversión. Tras recorrer las calles reinadas por una oscuridad absoluta, la luz se hacía en los *night-clubs* y los restaurantes, donde el negocio iba viento en popa.

El mundo se sumió en la era atómica en agosto de 1945, cuando los Aliados lanzaron la primera bomba nuclear sobre Hiroshima. Un mes más tarde, la rendición de los japoneses puso fin a la guerra en el Pacífico y el júbilo de la victoria impulsó a la población a consumir y a conducir. Entre 1946 y 1950 se vendieron 21,4 millones de automóviles. En 1949, la producción alcanzó los cinco millones de vehículos por primera vez en la historia. De los 222.862 automóviles fabricados en 1943 se ascendió a 2.148.699 en 1946, de los que General Motors vendió 1.240.418.

En 1946, el automóvil, convertido en el nuevo símbolo de la libertad y la independencia, permitía a los estadounidenses recorrer su país de costa a costa.

Con todo, los viajes más lujosos eran los que se hacían en tren o en crucero. Para quienes tenían miedo a las alturas, nada era comparable a la elegancia del *Queen Elizabeth*, que cubría la ruta de Nueva York a Portsmouth con las máximas comodidades, o los vagones de Pullman, que no envidiaban nada a los cruceros de lujo.

El sueño americano de posguerra se originó con el proyecto de ley para excomba-
tientes G. I. Bill, que puso a disposición de los veteranos de guerra viviendas
asequibles. Se llevó a cabo el primer plan para la construcción de casas pre-
fabricadas aplicando una tecnología de fabricación similar a la de la industria
automovilística. Se inició así el movimiento migratorio que llevó a la población
a trasladarse de las ciudades a las afueras, y se produjo un *boom* en la natalidad.
En 1947 se batió el número de nacimientos con 3,8 millones de alumbramientos,
cifra que a finales de la década había alcanzado los 32 millones, superando en ocho
millones el récord de la década anterior. Como consecuencia, las industrias de
pañales y preparados para lactantes proliferaron en Estados Unidos.

En 1946, Hollywood retomó la actividad que mejor se le daba: hacer buenas
películas. En un año el cine y la radio se vieron amenazados por una inno-
vación revolucionaria: la televisión. Las familias estadounidenses se sentaban
frente a los televisores Motorola o Zenith con la comida sobre el regazo para
ver sus programas preferidos. Pese a todo, *Reader's Digest* continuó siendo la
revista más popular de Estados Unidos, con nueve millones de ejemplares vendi-
dos en 1949, seguida por *Life Magazine*, con 5.305.394 ejemplares.

La comida enlatada penetró en los hogares estadounidenses al finalizar la guerra. Cajas de cereales,
como la de Kellogg's, preguntaban al consumidor: «¿Le ha cambiado la guerra los hábitos del
desayuno?». La comida enlatada nació con Spam, la ración de jamón enlatada que se enviaba a los
militares durante la guerra.

Durante los años cuarenta, los anuncios de tabaco y bebidas alcohólicas contaron con la presencia de
algunas leyendas de la pantalla. Humphrey Bogart fumaba un Chesterfield y bebía un Chivas Regal en
Casablanca. Con todo descaro, Camel anunciaba: «Camel, el tabaco de los médicos», afirmación que
hoy atraería la atención del Ministerio de Salud. Durante la década de 1940, la industria tabacalera
vendió 300 millones de cigarrillos al año.

Al concluir la guerra, las empresas volvieron a inundar el mercado con productos de consumo. General
Electric vendía bombillas de 100 vatios a quince centavos. Kodak, que había inmortalizado las atroci-
dades de la guerra, documentaba ahora los tiempos de paz con familias disfrutando de barbacoas en
el jardín o reuniones familiares por Navidad.

A finales de la década, una ola de prosperidad económica alcanzó a Estados Unidos. No obstante,
el fin de una guerra sólo supuso el principio de otra. La adquisición por parte de
Rusia de una bomba atómica avivó el fuego de la Guerra Fría, que durante años
enfrentó a la Unión Soviética y a Estados Unidos. El miedo a que estallara una
guerra nuclear se hizo omnipresente. Hacia los años cincuenta, los niños prac-
ticaban simulacros de ataque aéreo escondiéndose bajo sus pupitres, y los ciu-
dadanos de a pie cavaban refugios atómicos en los patios de sus casas
preparándose para la guerra de una forma nunca vista en suelo americano.

食料配給制から繁栄へ：1940年代のアメリカン・ライフ

ウィリー・R・ウィルカーソン3世

時は1941年。アメリカは戦時下にあり、午後6時以降は消灯管制が敷かれていた。

その前年には、オールズモビル社が「世界一モダンな車」を作り出したと高らかに宣言したばかりだった。しかし、今や自動車メーカーは、102,351台の戦車と、2,455,964台という途方もない数のトラックをアメリカ陸軍向けに製造するために工場の設備を再編成していた。女たちは、彼女たちの夫や恋人を前線に送り込むだろう爆撃機の部品を組み立てていた。

多くの企業が戦争努力に不可欠な製品を作る方向に転換する中、コカ・コーラ社が「我々は品質に忠実です」と表明すれば、チェスターフィールド社は「ここから勝利に」と消費者を駆り立てた。

戦争初期、東海岸沿いでは記録的な数のアメリカ商船がドイツのUボート群によって沈められていた。米陸軍省は、信憑性のない話に耳を貸さないよう、国民に警告するためのポスターを制作した。沈みゆく船の絵の下に「軽口が船を沈没させる」というスローガンが記されたポスターはそこここに——バス停から路面電車のターミナルまで——掲示された。

アメリカの強大な軍事力は戦争債の存在抜きには語れない。戦争努力を鼓舞しようと、映画業界は長編映画の代わりにプロパガンダ映画の製作を行う機関となっていたのだ。映画監督フランク・キャプラは『我々はなぜ戦うのか』と題されたシリーズを撮り、戦争プロパガンダの急先鋒となった。40年代においては、映画館で本編前に上映されていたパテ社の映画がそのままニュースにもなった。化粧品の代わりに制服を手に入れた映画スターたちは、戦争債の売上に貢献し、軍隊の階級に連なった。ボブ・ホープを筆頭メンバーに構成された米軍慰問協会による巡業は、戦地が渇望していた娯楽を提供し、兵士たちの士気を高める役割を担った。

その頃アメリカ国内では、食料やガソリンは配給制度であったにもかかわらず、人々は街に繰り出して楽しい時間を過ごしていた。消灯管制の下、暗い夜道を進むのは容易ではなかったが、ナイトクラブやレストランは別次元の話だった。商売はにわかに景気づいていた。

1945年8月、連合国軍による広島への初の原爆投下が世界に原子力時代の到来を告げた。その1ヶ月後、日本の降伏によって太平洋戦争が終戦を迎えると、アメリカと自動車との本格的な恋愛関係が始まった。勝利によってもたらされた歓喜が、人々を熱狂的な消費と運転に向かわせたのだ。1946年から1950年の間に、2,140万台の新車が販売された。1949年には、年間生産数が初めて500万台の大台を超えた。1943年には222,862台だった乗用車の生産台数が1946年には2,148,699台へと跳ね上がり、そのうちゼネラル・モーターズ社が最大シェアを誇る1,240,418台を売った。

1946年には、自動車はアメリカの自由と独立を象徴する存在となっていた。この、新たに手に入れた自由の表現によって、戦後のアメリカ人は、国中を縦横無尽にドライブしてまわることができた。より贅沢な旅は、列車や船によって提供された。空を飛ぶことに恐怖を覚える向きには、ニューヨークからポーツマスまで一流の旅を保証してくれるクイーン・エリザベス2世号の優雅さに勝るものはなかったし、プルマン・カーはその客船にも劣らない豪華な列車だった。アメリカの荒野を勢いよく走るペンシルバニア鉄道は、「ここはいつでも良いお天気…」と宣伝していた。

戦後のアメリカン・ドリームの原点は復員兵援護法にある。手頃な価格で家を入手する機会が初めて復員軍人に対して与えられたのだ。その頃、ニューヨークのビジネスマン、ウィリアム・J・レヴィットは、主に自動車工場などで活用されていた生産ラインを家作りに応用するというアイデアを思いついていた。レヴィットは、初の組み立て式住宅街を開発し、戦後の都市から郊外への人口移動の先鞭をつけた。

　1947年には、過去最高の記録となった380万人の新生児が生まれ、40年代を通じての合計出生数も3,200万人と、30年代の記録を800万人も上回った。おむつや乳幼児用ミルク産業は大繁盛だった。

　1946年、ハリウッドは、彼らがもっとも得意とする仕事に戻った——映画を作ることだ。そして供給が不足することはなかった。しかし1年も経たぬうちに、映画とラジオは共にある革命的な新技術の脅威にさらされることになった。テレビの登場である。アメリカの家族はダイニングルームを見捨て、代わりに皿を膝の上に乗せてモトローラやゼニスの前に集まっては、お気に入りのテレビ番組を見るようになった。「リーダーズ・ダイジェスト」誌はアメリカを代表する雑誌でありつづけ、1949年には900万部を販売している。その年の売上で第2位に入ったのは「ライフ」誌で、販売部数は5,305,394部だった。

　缶詰などのコンビニエンスフードは戦時中に登場し、戦争が終わるとともに一般家庭に普及した。ケロッグ社の「コーンフレーク」のような箱入りシリアルは広告でこう問いかけた。「戦争が朝食の習慣をめちゃくちゃにしていませんか？」今やアメリカの食生活を代表するものとなった缶詰だが、原点は戦時中にGIに支給された缶入りハムの「スパム」にある。

　1940年代、アルコールとタバコの広告は伝説の映画スターたちの十八番だった。カサブランカのリックの店でチェスターフィールドを吸い、シーバスリーガルを呷るハンフリー・ボガートのように。キャメルは大胆にも「多くの医者がキャメルを吸っている」と、今だったらすぐさま医務総監に目をつけられそうな広告を打っている。1940年代を通して、彼らは毎年3億本のタバコを販売し、1950年までの10年間の合計売上は3億5,730万ドルに上った。

　戦後、各社が軍需品から消費者製品の製造へと切り替えたことで、街には商品があふれかえった。ゼネラル・エレクトリック社は100ワットの電球を1個15セントで販売した。戦争の残虐さをとらえたコダックのフィルムは、今では平時の娯楽、裏庭での夏のバーベキューやクリスマスの集まりを記録するものになった。家の中では冷蔵庫が必要不可欠だった。

　40年代も終盤にさしかかって、アメリカは、目覚しい技術革新が拍車をかけた、けた違いの経済的繁栄を経験した。しかし、一つの戦争の終わりはまた新たな戦争の始まりでもあった。ソ連とアメリカの間の冷戦は、その後数十年間に及ぶ猫と鼠の追っかけあいに火をつけ、ゲームはソ連が原爆を手にした時に現実のものとなった。核戦争の恐怖はかつてないほど拡がった。それは学校の中にまでも及んだ。1950年代は、子供たちが空襲に備えるため避難訓練で机の下に隠れたり、一般市民が家庭に防空壕を掘ったりするなど、アメリカ国内でありとあらゆる戦争準備をする時代となる。

Gracious
as the Old South

From the four corners of the globe are gathered gracious flavors to lend bouquet to this fine gin. Dixie Belle has that clean, suave taste that makes it mingle agreeably without over-emphasis in your favorite gin drinks. The gin preferred above all by those who appreciate the ultimate in quality.

—made from 100% grain

CONTINENTAL DISTILLING
CORPORATION, Phila., Pa.
90 PROOF • DISTILLED FROM 100% GRAIN NEUTRAL SPIRITS

Calvert Whiskey & Gin, 1941 ◄◄ *Gilbey's Gin, 1941* ◄ *Dixie Belle Gin, 1944*

CARLING'S

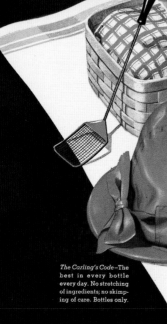

The Carling's Code—The best in every bottle every day. No stretching of ingredients; no skimping of care. Bottles only.

You can tell it's a picnic—for there's that Red Cap!

Carling's, you know, is...<u>Light</u>—not logy...<u>Mellow</u>—not musty ...<u>Better</u>—not bitter

...all the result of Carling's unique and exclusive method of cross-blending in the vat.

Like beer? Like ale? Take along Carling's!

Now at the same price as premium beers.

BREWING CORPORATION OF AMERICA, Cleveland, Ohio

BORN IN CANADA (1840). NOW GOING GREAT IN THE 48 STATES AS A PRODUCT OF U. S. A.

Carling's Red Cap Ale, 1947

THANKSGIVING 1942

AMERICA *Makes the Best* OF EVERYTHING!

Americans—this Thanksgiving—welcome the privilege of "all-out" effort. Schenley, on a war footing, does its part by using its vast facilities to make War alcohol. The Schenley Royal Reserve you enjoy today is drawn from our reserves—the largest in the U.S.A.—made and laid down in years gone by, and blended with finest grain neutral spirits for perfect mildness.

Drink **SCHENLEY** *Royal Reserve*

THE TASTE IT TAKES FOUR STATES TO MAKE

Schenley Whiskey, 1942

There's nothing like it...

absolutely nothing

Out of the bracing cold, into the cheery warmth ... an open fire crackles an invitation to relax. And Budweiser completes the picture. Its exquisite bouquet escaping through the creamy foam is a clue to the distinctive taste. Live life, every golden minute of it. Enjoy Budweiser, every golden drop of it.

ANHEUSER-BUSCH
ST. LOUIS

Budweiser

TRADE MARK REG. U. S. PAT. OFF.

World-famous because of the cost and quality of its ingredients, superior brewing methods and inimitable taste.

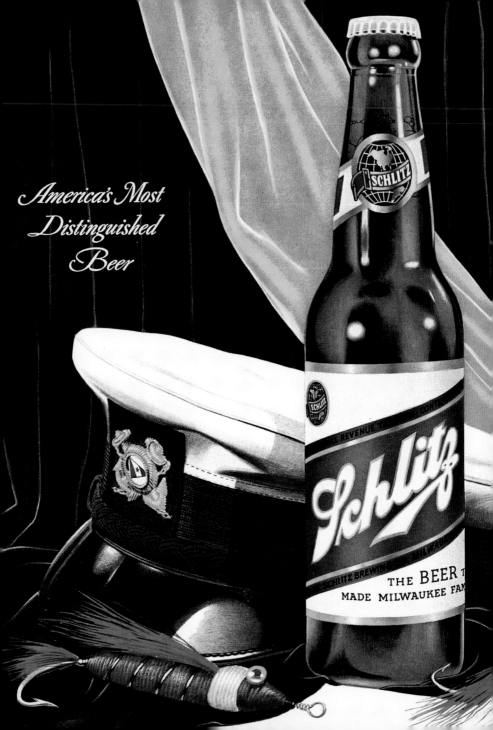

"Streamlined smoking!—a basic new design, Colonel!"

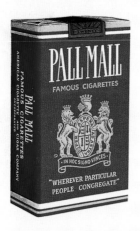

● HERE'S THE MOST important cigarette improvement in 25 years—streamlined smoking.

It's Pall Mall—a cigarette deliberately designed for better smoking! Pall Mall is over 20 per cent longer than the old-style cigarette. And this additional length is important.

Because it travels the smoke further—the smoke reaches you cooler. Because it filters the smoke through more tobacco—the smoke is definitely milder.

Important, too, is BULKING.

Because this careful Pall Mall process

mellows tobaccos as nothing else can.

In BULKING, the traditionally fine Pall Mall tobaccos acquire a new character. The delicate flavors blend together. All harshness is gradually softened. Pall Mall becomes a noticeably smoother cigarette.

The smoke of these fine tobaccos—enriched by BULKING, traveled and filtered through Pall Mall's greater length—gives you a combination of advantages no other cigarette can offer.

"Streamlined smoking!—a basic new design, Colonel!"

Prove it! Yourself, try Pall Mall critically.

"WHEREVER PARTICULAR PEOPLE CONGREGATE"

Chesterfield, 1940 ◄   *Pall Mall Cigarettes, 1941*

Chesterfield, 1941

And the winner is...

It's a Fact — A Warm Wonderful Fact

What better endorsement for lighting up than knowing that your personal physician was enjoying the same pleasure of the rich flavor of "Camels costlier tobaccos"? With over 100,000 doctors surveyed in 1946, logic assumed cigarette smoking was a harmless habit. Health hazard? Who cared. Your T (taste) zone would let you know how cigarettes affected your throat. And, of course, your doctor's nicotine habit would sooth any qualms about the safety of smoking. If your doctor smoked, why not you?

Wenn guter Rat gefragt ist

Was wäre ermutigender, sich eine anzustecken, als das Wissen, dass auch der eigene Hausarzt dem Genuss von »Camels ausgewählten Tabaksorten« frönt? Da die Statistik 1946 über 100.000 rauchende Ärzte aufwies, legte es die Logik nahe, dass Rauchen harmlos sei. Gesundheitliche Risiken? Ach was. Die Geschmackspapillen würden einen schon wissen lassen, wie sich Zigaretten auf die Schleimhäute auswirken. Und natürlich sollte der Nikotinkonsum des eigenen Arztes jegliche Bedenken über die Ungefährlichkeit des Rauchens ausräumen. Denn wenn mein Arzt raucht, warum dann nicht ich?

Une réalité chaude et encourageante !

Pour s'accorder le plaisir d'en griller une, existe-t-il de meilleure garantie que celle de votre médecin affirmant que lui aussi connaît cet immense plaisir d'une « Camel, la plus riche des blondes » ? Lors d'une enquête en 1946, plus de 100 000 médecins le confirment, ce qui semble logiquement prouver que fumer ne nuit pas à la santé. Y a-t-il risque sanitaire ? Qu'importe ? Votre sens du goût vous dira en quoi fumer affecte votre gorge. De toutes façons, le fait que votre médecin s'adonne à la nicotine devrait faire taire tous vos scrupules et vos inquiétudes. Puisque lui fume, pourquoi pas vous ?

La pura y cálida realidad

¿Qué mejor aval para encender un cigarrillo que saber que nuestro médico de cabecera también disfruta del placer de un «Camel, el rubio más suave»? Una encuesta realizada en 1946 confirmaba que más de cien mil doctores fumaban, lo cual llevaba a pensar, por lógica, que fumar era un hábito inofensivo. ¿Un peligro para la salud? ¿Quién se lo planteaba? Las fosas nasales y la garganta, la llamada «zona T», ya se encargaban de avisarnos de cuándo un cigarrillo nos hacía daño. Y, por descontado, la adicción a la nicotina de nuestro médico disipaba cualquier duda sobre si fumar era perjudicial o no. Si él fumaba, ¿por qué no íbamos a hacerlo nosotros?

事実です——暖かく素晴らしい事実

かかりつけの内科医や外科医が「贅沢なタバコ、キャメル」の豊かな味を吸い込む喜びを、あなたと同じように享受していると言うのならば、タバコの広告としてこれ以上の宣伝文句はないだろう。1946年に行われた、10万人以上の医者を対象とした調査の結果から、論理的には喫煙は無害な習慣だと位置づけられた。健康への害だって？かまうものか。あなたのT（＝味覚）ゾーンが、タバコが喉にどう作用したかを教えてくれるはず。それにもちろん、あなたのドクターのニコチン常習が、喫煙の安全性に関して時折首をもたげてくる不安をなだめてくれるだろう。医者が吸っているのに、やめる必要ありますか？

"I'm going to grow a hundred years old!"

...and possibly she may—for the amazing strides of medical science have added years to life expectancy

● It's a fact—a warm and wonderful fact—that this five-year-old child, or your own child, has a life expectancy almost a whole decade longer than was her mother's, and a good 18 to 20 years longer than that of her grandmother. Not only the expectation of a longer life, but of a life by far healthier.

Thank medical science for that. Thank your doctor and thousands like him...toiling ceaselessly, often with little or no public recognition...that you and yours may enjoy a longer, better life.

According to a recent Nationwide survey:

More Doctors smoke Camels
than any other cigarette!

NOT ONE but three outstanding independent research organizations conducted this survey. And they asked not just a few thousand, but 113,597, doctors from coast to coast to name the cigarette they themselves preferred to smoke.

The answers came in by the thousands...from general physicians, diagnosticians, surgeons—yes, and nose and throat specialists too. The most-named brand was Camel.

If you are not now smoking Camels, try them. Compare them critically. See how the full, rich flavor of Camel's costlier tobaccos suits your taste. See how the cool mildness of a Camel suits your throat. Let your "T-Zone" tell you (*see right*).

THE "T-ZONE" TEST WILL TELL YOU

The "T-Zone"—T for taste and T for throat—is your own proving ground for any cigarette. Only your taste and throat can decide which cigarette tastes best to you...how it affects your throat. On the basis of the experience of many, many millions of smokers, we believe Camels will suit your "T-Zone" to a "T"

R. J. Reynolds Tobacco Co.
Winston-Salem, N. C.

CAMELS *Costlier Tobaccos*

CAMEL
TURKISH & DOMESTIC BLEND CIGARETTES

so wide—so deep!
And beautifully tailored, too! I wish I could get the Ford people to do over our sofa. I've never seen better looking upholstery—nor better needlework!

Looks that last!
My husband says Ford's beauty comes from "baked enamel." Maybe that's why the finish has that wonderful feel of my pet service plates . . . and they were wedding presents!

Ford's out front with *Mrs. America!*

I'm bustin' with pride!
Our new Ford is the best-looking thing in town. And that "Lifeguard" body gives me a feeling of safety I've never had with any other car—and that's important to a mother!

THERE'S A *Ford* IN YOUR FUTURE

So Smooth—So Quiet
Our Ford Dealer told us it has a 100-horsepower V-8 engine but frankly you'd hardly know the car has an engine at all—it's so quiet! (That's right, Lady, and so's the 90-horsepower Ford Six!—Ed.)

Step into this New Chrysler and Fluid Drive away for the motoring thrill of a lifetime!

Do yourself a favor…try Chrysler's *Fluid Drive.* See how much easier it is…how much smoother it is…how much simpler, safer, pleasanter! Why shift gears? Why pump a clutch? Why buy a new car and still have to drive the old-fashioned way? A Chrysler dealer near you is eager to give you a treat. Please 'phone him! **BE MODERN**

Buy Chrysler!

WITH FLUID DRIVE AND VACAMATIC TRANSMISSION

INTERNATIONAL *Trucks*

NEW HEAVY-DUTY POWER, PERFORMANCE, ECONOMY

The new cabs are designed for high-way safety, driver-efficiency and driver-comfort. Foam-type rubber seat cushion, adjustable seat back, generous head and leg room. All-steel construction, safety glass all around.

HERE'S a new view of America's *favorite** heavy-duty truck—completely redesigned and geared for the extraordinary demands of 1941. This year, trucks and the highways on which they roll assume a new importance in the nation's No. 1 job—National Defense. The New Internationals—product of 34 years of truck-manufacturing experience—are superbly fitted for today's transportation needs.

One look and you recognize modern streamline styling at its best. Put these new Internationals to work on your job, and you get a new idea of *performance, power* and *stamina*—and *unbelievable operating economy.*

These new K-Line Internationals have

new Hi-Tork hydraulic brakes for smooth straight-line stops, under full load—no grabbing, fading or squealing. New, easier steering for greater safety and tireless handling. New, improved frame construction; new, rugged rear axles; and new, longer, easy-riding springs. And even more important, there are powerful, 6-cylinder, valve-in-head engines designed and built by International to lick the toughest jobs— with power to spare.

The new International line includes all sizes from the ½-ton delivery up to powerful 6-wheel and Diesel-powered units. Write for catalog.

INTERNATIONAL HARVESTER COMPANY
180 North Michigan Ave.   Chicago, Illinois

> **FREE Movie—"Singing Wheels"**
> Thrilling 22-minute feature produced by Motor Truck Committee, Automobile Manufacturers Association. Now ready for club and organization meetings. Write to Harvester.

* For ten years more heavy-duty Internationals have

NEW CHEVROLET TRUCKS

MOST POWERFUL of all low-priced trucks

C17-96
19 IIICLI 41

174 FOOT-POUNDS TORQUE
90-Horsepower Standard Engine

192 FOOT-POUNDS TORQUE
93-Horsepower Heavy Duty "Load-Master" Engine (*Available at extra cost on Heavy Duty trucks*)

These new Chevrolet trucks are the most modern, most comfortable, most popular low-priced trucks you can buy.

Trucks with Passenger Car Steering Ease by the World's Leading Truck Builder

60 models on nine longer wheelbases ···a complete line for all lines of business

CHEVROLET MOTOR DIVISION, General Motors Sales Corporation, DETROIT, MICHIGAN

OUT-PULL ··· OUT-VALUE ··· OUT-SELL

FINEST OF THE FAMOUS

"Silver Streaks"

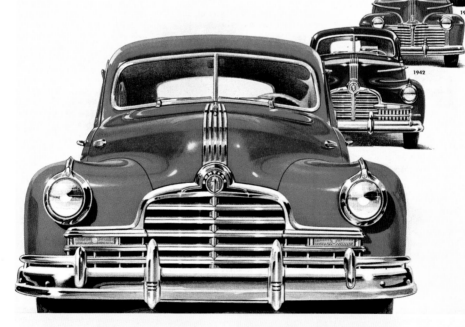

This is the new Pontiac—a car that adds new luster to a fine old name. It carries to an even higher level the tradition of quality that began when the first Pontiac "Silver Streak" was introduced a decade ago. If you are a Pontiac owner you know what that statement means— because four years of wartime driving have proved that Pontiac quality pays great dividends in owner satisfaction. And if you have never owned a Pontiac, we believe you will be greatly impressed by this fine new car. In appearance, in all-around performance, in comfort—*in everything that stands for quality—* it is the finest of the famous "Silver Streaks."

1935
1936
1937
1938
1939
194
1941
1942

NEW PONTIAC

PONTIAC MOTOR DIVISION • GENERAL MOTORS CORPORATION

Pontiac, 1945

▶ *Plymouth, 1940*

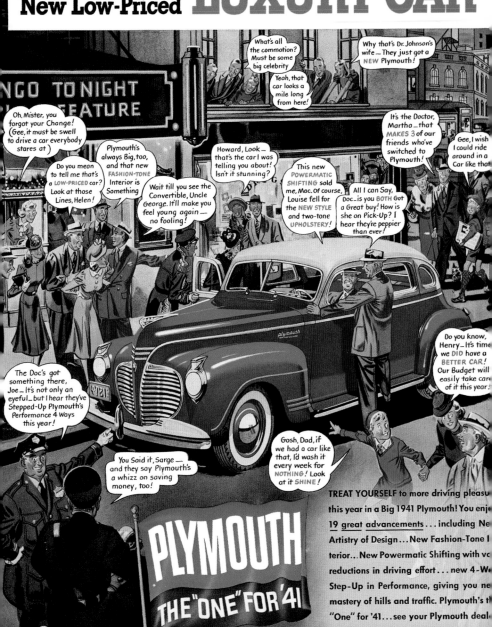

Ahead... *Your Chrysler gives you the new, the exciting* ... *but with more*
protection than you ever had before. From new Safety rim wheels to Safe-guard
hydraulic brakes, Chrysler engineers balance each advance in making it more
fun to drive, with advances that make the beautiful Chrysler safer to drive.

From coast to coast, see a Chrysler-Plymouth dealer for finest service.

the Beautiful Chrysler

WITH HYDRAULICALLY
OPERATED TRANSMISSION
AND gyrol FLUID DRIVE

Chrysler, 1945

Studebaker Land Cruiser

All eyes are on this "next look" in cars!

AMERICA EXPECTS the unexpected from Studebaker—and here it is—the "next look" in cars!

This is a truly inspired 1950 Studebaker—dynamically new in form and substance—styled ahead and engineered ahead for years to come.

A breath-taking new Studebaker Champion in the low-price field—a value-packed new Studebaker Commander—in your choice of dreamlined sedans, coupes and convertibles! An ultra-luxurious special Land Cruiser sedan, too!

Stop in and see these new 1950 Studebaker thrill cars first chance you have. See for yourself why Studebaker's really rolling! Studebaker leads again with the "next look" in cars!

White sidewall tires and wheel discs optional at extra co

America likes this "next look" in interiors —Fabulously fine nylon cord upholstery, introduced into motoring by Studebaker, is standard in the 1950 Land Cruiser and regal de luxe Commander. Land Cruiser is shown.

America likes Studebaker gas economy —Studebaker's higher compression Champion and Commander engines of increased horsepower use gasoline very sparingly. Automatic overdrive is available at extra cost.

America likes Studebaker's new driving thrill—Every 1950 Studebaker handles with light-touch ease—rides so smoothly it almost completely abolishes travel fatigue. A new kind of coil spring front suspension.

America likes Studebaker craftsmanshi —Men of conscience and competence, man of them father-and-son teams, build surviv ing soundness into every 1950 Studebaker

© 1949, The Studebaker Corp'n, South Bend 27, Indiana, U.S.,

Studebaker, 1949

Winter Adventure in Fireside Comfort—

...in the NEW FRAZER!

See and drive the new 1949 FRAZER Manhattan —"The pride of Willow Run"

Take off into a frosty wonderland in the car that's engineered for year 'round comfort and enjoyment. Thermometer show zero? Doesn't matter. Thanks to the FRAZER air conditioner, winter's lost its sting. You touch a button—and make your weather as you go—nestled in fireside comfort—free from the searching wind. Here's another product of FRAZER research—a whole car full of clean circulating air—warm in winter, cool in summer—a complete change every minute. Yes, the new FRAZER is rugged and dependable—for all-weather, all-season...adventure. See your dealer today!

PONTIAC

MOTOR CARS

ANOTHER FEATHER ...

Always Drive Carefully

Out of the difficult years of the war has emerged another important distinction for Pontiac: *Its owners report that Pontiac exceeded even their own high expectations from the standpoint of dependability and generally satisfactory performance.* Their praise is extremely gratifying. Many owners say that from all practical standpoints—their Pontiacs are as satisfactory today as they were at the time of Pearl Harbor. We hope that America's cars will never again be put to the test they were called upon to survive in the four long years of war. But, such a reserve of quality as the Pontiac car has revealed is a most valuable asset under any condition of usage. It means an extra measure of economy and satisfaction throughout all the years of your ownership.

PONTIAC MOTOR DIVISION of GENERAL MOTORS CORPORATION

Frazier, 1949 ◄ Pontiac, 1946

IT PAYS TO BE *Far-Sighted*

THE NEW GENERAL SQUEEGEE CUSHION . . . with 24 lbs. of air . . . is luxuriously buoyant and silent at any speed you would travel. Its softer ride creates an entirely new conception of relaxed motoring. And there is a new feeling of complete security in the way it holds the road . . . and around curves without a trace of weave. In extra long, safe mileage . . . and for the quickest action-traction stops, rain or shine, it surpasses the finest tire we have ever built.

SOFTER RIDING

MORE MILEAGE

QUICKER STOPS

The **GENERAL** SQUEEGEE

—goes a long way to make friends

© 1948.
THE GENERAL TIRE & RUBBER CO., AKRON

General Tire, 1948 ▶ *Firestone, 1940* ▶▶ *United States Rubber Company, 1945*

Firestone
CHAMPION TIRES

FOR 21 CONSECUTIVE YEARS FIRESTONE TIRES HAVE BEEN ON ALL THE WINNING CARS IN THE 500-MILE INDIANAPOLIS RACE

FLASHING down the straightaways at speeds as high as 160 miles an hour, Wilbur Shaw streaked to victory in this great race to become a three-time winner and the only man ever to win two consecutive victories at Indianapolis.

500 miles of grinding, pounding, torturing speed—and not one tire failed! Here's proof of Safety—Proof of Blowout Protection—Proof of Tire Superiority—backed, not by claims, but by **performance.**

Patented construction features in the Firestone Tires used by these great drivers on the speedway are incorporated in the Firestone Champion Tires you buy for the highway.

For greater safety, economy and dependability, equip **your** car with a set of these wonderful tires today. Easy terms on the Firestone Budget Plan if you desire.

Listen to the "Voice of Firestone," Monday evenings, N.B.C. Red Network.

See Firestone Champion Tires made in Firestone Factory and Exhibition Building at the New York World's Fair

THE ONLY TIRES MADE THAT ARE SAFETY-PROVED ON THE SPEEDWAY FOR YOUR PROTECTION ON THE HIGHWAY

And the winner is...

See it Spinning at High Speeds Backwards!

Does anyone still think that the innovative auto designers of the 1940s hadn't given a thought to safety? Apparently the creators of the Davis did, with their short-lived experiment of the post-war period. This pocket-sized three wheeler was designed for disaster. Never mind seat belts. Four American Airlines stewardesses had plenty of safety room. Or so the ad claimed. Speeding backwards and forwards at high speeds? No problem. The Davis could stop on a dime. Hang onto your hats and write your will, the Davis is here!

Mit Vollgas rückwärts um die eigene Achse!

Wer sagte noch, die innovativen Autodesigner der Vierziger hätten nicht an Sicherheit gedacht? Offenbar galt dies den Entwicklern des Davis, eines kurzlebigen Nachkriegsexperiments. Das Dreiradgefährt im Taschenformat war auf ein Fiasko zugeschnitten. Anschnallgurte konnte man getrost vergessen. Vier Stewardessen der American Airlines hatten hier jede Menge Sicherheitsabstand. So jedenfalls behauptete es die Werbung. Mit Vollgas in den Rückwärts- oder Vorwärtsgang? Kein Problem. Der Davis kam auf einer Münze zum Stehen. Halt alles fest und schreib dein Testament, hier kommt der Davis!

A toute berzingue en marche arrière !

Qui a dit que la sécurité n'intéressait pas les jeunes designers des années 40 ? Sans doute les créateurs de la Davis, produit à l'existence brève. Cette trois roues, au format de poche, est une véritable catastrophe. Et pas question de ceintures de sécurité. Quatre hôtesses de l'air peuvent y vaquer à leur aise, affirme la pub. Foncer à toute berzingue en marche avant ou arrière ? Aucun problème. La Davis peut piler au centimètre près. Accrochez-vous ferme et partez l'âme en paix. La Davis s'occupe du reste.

¡A toda velocidad y marcha atrás!

¿Quién ha dicho que los innovadores diseñadores d e automóviles de los años cuarenta no prestaban atención a las cuestiones de seguridad? Aparentemente, los creadores del Davis sí lo hicieron en un experimento de existencia efímera aparecido en la posguerra. Este vehículo de tres ruedas y tamaño de bolsillo estaba concebido para abocarnos al desastre. De nada servían los cinturones de seguridad. La publicidad afirmaba que había espacio suficiente para cuatro azafatas de American Airlines. ¿Que se alcanzaban velocidades vertiginosas marcha adelante o marcha atrás? Ningún problema. El Davis era capaz de detenerse en seco. Agárrese el sombrero y haga testamento: ¡el Davis ya está aquí!

ハイスピードで後ろ向きに回転するところを見てください!

1940年代の革新的なカー・デザイナーたちは、安全性のことなど考えもしなかったと、まだそうお考えだろうか。戦後期の短命な実験に終わったデイヴィスの作り手たちは、明らかにそのことについて考えたようだ。この小型三輪車は大惨事に遭うために設計されている。シートベルトなんかどうでもいい。アメリカン航空の4人のスチュワーデスたちには十分な安全スペースが確保されている。というのが広告の主張である。後方、前方ともにハイスピードで疾走できるかって? お安いご用だ。デイヴィスはすぐにきちっと停止する。しっかりつかまったら、遺書を書かなければ。デイヴィスが来るぞ!

You saw it at the Pasadena Tournament of Roses...

You read about it in LIFE...in thousands of magazines and newspapers

*Four American Airlines Stewardesses
demonstrate the roomy comfort of the new Davis*

Now!
SEE THE DAVIS
IN ACTION!

SEE IT spinning at high speeds backwards
and forwards in a thirteen foot circle . . . .

SEE IT "stopping on-a-dime". . . .

SEE ITS amazing "painless parking" in less
space than needed by other full-sized cars

FREE PUBLIC DEMONSTRATIONS FOR 10 DAYS!

You are cordially invited to the First Open House
Demonstration of the new Davis 3-Wheeler—at our Assembly
Plant, 8055 Woodley Avenue, Van Nuys.

Demonstrations every hour on the hour from 9 A.M. to 9 P.M.
—rain or shine—starting Tuesday, January 27th, through
February 5th—Saturday and Sunday included.

HOW TO GET TO THE DAVIS PLANT

MOTORCAR COMPANY

Davis, 1948

PRESENTING

LAUNDERALL

The Completely Automatic HOME LAUNDRY

Launderall

Better-built to do a better job! **by Jacobs**

Nationally distributed by 5,000 carefully selected dealers

BETTER WASHING RESULTS—are assured with Launderall's Re-Verso-Rol washing action. Cylinder reverses direction 4 times a minute—dropping clothes gently through sudsy water with no tangling.

NO BENDING OR STOOPING—You load and unload clothes through Launderall's waist-high, Top-Fil-Dor. Since the door is on top, clothes can be added or removed during operating cycles.

SAFE FOR TOTS—The Safti-Latch automatically shuts off Launderall when Top-Fil-Dor is opened—protecting inquisitive fingers and careless hands against injury. There are no exposed moving parts.

READY FOR THE LINE—Launderall's Roto-Drier spin-dries clothes thoroughly—even heavy seams won't drip—yet its gentle action is safe for delicate fabrics—harmless to buttons, fasteners.

Imagine—your washing being merely a matter of flicking a switch! For that's all you do after putting soiled clothes and soap in Launderall through the handy Top-Fil-Dor—Launderall does it all for you, automatically—washes, rinses, and spin-dries laundry ready for the line.

But there are other features of this sensational washer that you will be equally delighted with. Its Re-Verso-Rol washing action washes and rinses more thoroughly and gently. Its extra large capacity—its quiet, efficient performance, its modern-styled beauty—these and other outstanding features are causing countless women to turn to Launderall—the completely automatic home laundry.

F. L. JACOBS CO., DETROIT 1, MICHIGAN
Plants in Detroit, Grand Rapids, Traverse City, Holly, Mancelona, Mich., Indianapolis, Ind., Danville, Ill.

"Oh Mother!" cried Alice

"Here's the New **PHILCO**...

Deepfreeze

TRADE-MARK REG. U.S. PAT. OFF.

the talked—about home freezer

Opens at the top . . .
cold can't spill out
and isn't it a clean,
white beauty!

If he wants fish, if he wants meat, if he wants biscuits, pie, soup, orange juice, cake, strawberries, ice cream, or asparagus— why, just reach in the Deepfreeze and suit his (or your) fancy.

More food—more kinds of food—better food—in your home at all times, at lower cost.

Shop only when you feel like it. Buy in quantity when prices are right, and eat when you please.

Big enough for a large family, yet good business for even a family of two (more than 9 cubic feet—and every inch for food; holding more than 320 pounds). Costs no more to run than an ordinary electric refrigerator.

Yes—Deepfreeze is the leader in this modern age of home freezing. More units already in use (the proved home freezer). Most talked-about for what it will do.

For the small home and where space is limited, the economy-size Deepfreeze with more than 125 pounds capacity.

If you don't know the name of nearest Deepfreeze dealer, write us direct.

The cold goes round and round

Food is "wrapped" in a blanket of zero cold in the Deepfreeze. No food is farther than nine inches from the all-surrounding source of cold.

DEEPFREEZE DIVISION • MOTOR PRODUCTS CORPORATION • NORTH CHICAGO, ILLINOIS

Philco Refrigerator, 1948 ◄   Deepfreeze, 1946

Proctor Automatic Electric Appliances, 1945

▶ *Hoover Cleaner, 1946*

For every woman who is proud of her home

Get the cleaner you can be proud of to keep colors bright and rugs really clean.

The new Hoover 28 Cleaner is what women have been waiting for. It's the cleaner that saves your time and your strength. It has the easy operation you deserve. It has the fine name you want.

The Hoover is the 2 to 1 choice of women over any other cleaner. It has cleaning tools that plug in like magic. It has the price you'll appreciate.

See it at your dealers, or in your home.

HOOVER

THE HOOVER
REG. U. S. PAT. OFF.

IT BEATS • AS IT SWEEPS • AS IT CLEANS

THE HOOVER COMPANY, NORTH CANTON, OHIO
HAMILTON, ONTARIO, CANADA

A FIRST FLOOR WASHROOM *requires little space and adds much convenience . . . It simplifies child training, saves time for the whole family, reduces through-the-house traffic, provides handy facilities for your guests.*

CONTRIBUTING TO JOYOUS HEALTH

Good plumbing is of daily importance to your family's health. The quality of Kohler fixtures and fittings makes them an investment in safety, costing no more at first, and relieving you of worry and expense over the years.

Kohler fixtures are pleasing in line and proportion and have a smooth, lustrous hard surface that is easy to clean. Kohler fittings, of chromium-plated brass, have

the strength and precision that assure serviceability.

Your Kohler dealer will help you select the fixtures that will serve you best, in matched sets or individual pieces, for bathroom, kitchen, washroom, or laundry. Unified supervision watches over and coordinates every step of production, for Kohler products are made in one great plant. Write for Booklet 4SP, "Planned Bathrooms and Kitchens." Kohler Co., Kohler, Wis.

KOHLER OF KOHLER

PLUMBING FIXTURES AND FITTINGS • HEATING EQUIPMENT • ELECTRIC PLANTS

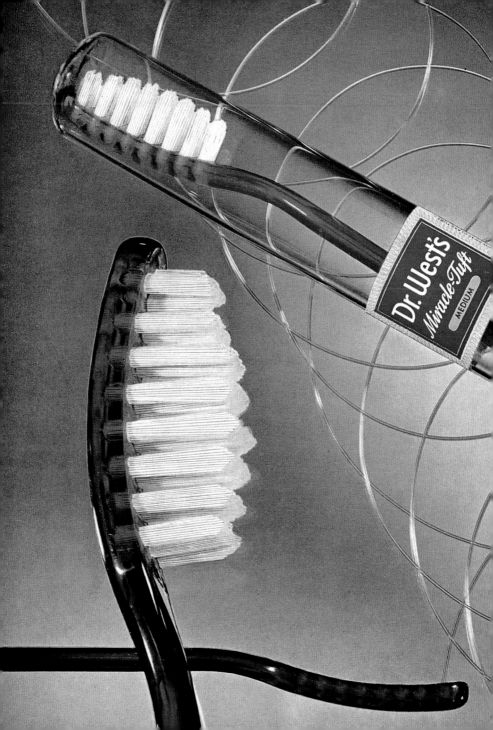

Kodak
TRADE-MARK

Cine-Kodak Magazine 8 Camera— 3-second magazine loading, fast, precision *f*/1.9 *Lumenized* lens, adjustable finder for standard and all accessory lenses, slow motion. $147.50. Also see **Cine-Kodak Reliant Camera.** Uses low-cost 8mm. roll film. Easy, sprocketless loading. With *f*/2.7 lens, $79; *f*/1.9 lens, $97.50.

Kodak Duaflex Camera—A 2¼ x 2¼ model with big "reflex" finder. Three stops: *f*/8, *f*/11, *f*/16. Double-exposure prevention. Kodar *f*/8 Lens. $19.85. With fixed-focus Kodet Lens, $12.75. Flasholder, $3.33. See also the popular Brownie Reflex Camera, $10.95.

More than ever,
a *Kodak Camera*
is the "wanted" *gift*

... Because nowadays even the simplest Kodak cameras make beautiful full-color pictures as well as black-and-white ... and with suitable accessory lighting all models shown operate right around the clock. See them at your Kodak dealer's.

Eastman Kodak Company, Rochester 4, N. Y.

All prices include Federal Tax

Kodak Tourist f/4.5 Camera— Kodak's finest 2¼ x 3¼ folding model. New 1/800 shutter, new-type release, built-in exposure guide. $95. With *f*/4.5 lens, 1/200 shutter, $71. With *f*/6.3 lens, $47.50; *f*/8.8 lens, $38.50; Kodet Lens, $24.50. Flasholder, $11.08.

Kodak Medalist II Camera—Finest lens in the 2¼ x 3¼ field—Kodak Ektar *f*/3.5. 1/400 shutter, coupled range finder, automatic film stop, depth-of-field scale. $312.50. Flasholder, $11.08.

Kodak Reflex II Camera— Kodak Ektalite Field Lens boosts image brightness 2½ times. Twin *f*/3.5 *Lumenized* lenses, 1/300 shutter, automatic film stop, improved field case. Negatives, 2¼ x 2¼. With field case, $155. Flasholder, $11.08.

Kodak 35 Camera with Range Finder—Popular choice for miniature Kodachrome photography. Speedy *f*/3.5 *Lumenized* lens, 1/200 shutter. Automatic shutter cocking, double-exposure prevention. $86.75. Flasholder, $11.08. Also see Kodak Retina I Camera, $72.75.

Gifts they'll use are fun to choose... exciting electric time by Telechron

$14.95 $9.95 $4.95 $5.95 $14.95 $7.95 $7.95 $57.95 $7.95 $6.95 $4.95 $32.00 $6.95 $4.95 $19.95 $37.00 $5.95 $19.95 $25.00 $5.95 $39.95★ $9.95

All prices plus tax. Prices and specifications subject to change without notice. Telechron Inc., Ashland, Mass. A General Electric Affiliate. ★ Includes tax. Price of Musalarm slightly higher in far west.

Telechron
REG. U.S. PAT. OFF.
ELECTRIC CLOCKS

"Lush"

"Swoony"

"Exquis"

Hmmmm . . . took the words right out of our mouth. Stream-lined them almost beyond recognition, too. But, generally speaking, that's what we were about to say of Pacific Sheets. They're so soft and smooth and so — well, yes, *lush*. So sleek and white and — *exquis*. So cool and caressing and — *swoony*.

And in any language Pacific Sheets are skilfully balanced — combining softness and smoothness with strength and wearing quality. The Pacific Factbook on each one gives you all the facts. Look for it when you shop.

BALANCED
PACIFIC
SHEETS

PACIFIC PERCALE · PACIFIC EXTRA-STRENGTH MUSLIN · PACIFIC TRUTH MUSLIN

FRANK SINATRA—sensational star of his own radio program, Wednesday nights over CBS.

GENERAL ELECTRIC PRESENTS

the First and Only

SELF-CHARGING PORTABLE RADIO

Here's a new portable that does what no other radio ever did before. It renews its battery power over and over again. It's self-charging.

No Battery Worries

Play it all you please with never a worry about the trouble and expense of regular battery replacements. Until you actually see and hear it you won't believe that any portable can be so smart, so light, so small. And still have such big-set performance—such big-set tone—such big-set power and selectivity.

Play it wherever you go—on picnics—on boats—on trains. Then indoors—just plug it in to AC house current. Even while you play this General Electric self-charging portable like any table set, the compact storage battery recharges for more hours of carefree entertainment anywhere.

Built Like A Battleship

Hear this amazing portable radio at your General Electric dealer's—now. See the beautiful plastic finish—the sturdy aluminum case. Open the back. You'll marvel at masterful engineering such as you never saw before in any radio. Tune in more stations with more power and clearer natural color tone than you get on most large sets. This G-E self-charging portable will be your prized companion—everywhere.

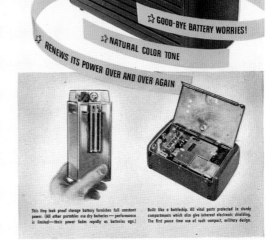

☆ GOOD-BYE BATTERY WORRIES!

☆ NATURAL COLOR TONE

☆ RENEWS ITS POWER OVER AND OVER AGAIN

GENERAL ⊛ ELECTRIC

LEADER IN RADIO, TELEVISION AND ELECTRONICS

RADIOS

This tiny leak proof storage battery furnishes full constant power. (All other portables use dry batteries — performance is limited—their power fades rapidly as batteries age.)

Built like a battleship. All vital parts protected in sturdy compartments which also give inherent electronic shielding. The first peace time use of such compact, military design.

GE **TELEVISION**

G-E Price Leader

Lowest priced G-E Television—yet no set made delivers more *quality* for $189.95.* Not an inch of wasted space in Model 805. Big 10" tube in an 11½" cabinet. It's practically *all picture!* Compact, rich rosewood plastic cabinet fits anywhere!

$189⁹⁵*

MODEL 821

BIG 12½" TUBE TABLE MODEL.
Lowest priced G-E Daylight Television—with BIG 12½" TUBE! *Daylight* bright, *daylight* clear, *daylight* sharp in a fully lighted room—no need to strain your eyes in darkness! Simplified tuning. Mahogany veneered cabinet. **Only $269.95***

MORE QUALITY
for your money...

Yᴇs, quality of picture ... of sound ... of style ... performance-engineered at Electronics Park. All three combine to make General Electric's great new Model 805 today's outstanding value in popular priced television. It brings you a screen nearly as wide as the cabinet itself! Your whole family enjoys big set pleasure ... easy tuning, long range reception, sharp, steady pictures. You get all these big set advantages at a surprisingly low price—plus an 87% saving in space. Ask your General Electric dealer to demonstrate this nationally acclaimed value.

General Electric Company, Electronics Park, Syracuse, N. Y.

*Plus tax, Installation extra. Prices slightly higher West and South—subject to change without notice.

You can put your confidence in—

GENERAL **GE** ELECTRIC

General Electric Television, 1949

She can be 5 places at once!

A fashion show in the eighth floor salon — and in four street windows at the same time! This is not a store manager's dream, but one way that television will serve, once the war is won.

It is not at all impossible that television equipment of many kinds will be developed for special and important uses in stores, factories, trains, schools — as well as homes.

This must wait, of course, for peace. Today all of Farnsworth's research, all of the skill and experience and knowledge gained through 16 years of development and manufacture are devoted to the production of superlative weapons and equipment for America's fighting men.

We cannot tell you much about this equipment — but we can say that progress is great. The radio and phonograph-radio you buy from Farnsworth tomorrow will reflect the advances being made today. So will the telecasting equipment we will be ready to furnish the studios in your locality. So, too, will the special television devices for industrial and educational purposes.

From the Farnsworth laboratories, in the past, have come many of the great discoveries which make electronic television a living reality. From Farnsworth, in the peacetime world of the future, will come a television receiving set for *your* home — ready, at the touch of a switch, to let you see the news and laughter, the art and science, of the world.

You can help bring that day of peace nearer — by buying today the War Bonds that are so vital to Victory.

E.C.Nicholas
President
Farnsworth Television & Radio Corporation, Fort Wayne, Indiana

FARNSWORTH TELEVISION

• Manufacturers of Radio and Television Transmitters and Receivers . . . Aircraft Radio Equipment . . . the Farnsworth Dissector Tube . . . the Capehart, the Capehart-Panamuse, and the Farnsworth Phonograph-Radios

PATTERN FOR...
Smart Living

Smart for family comfort—and for guests.

...WITH ECONOMY! *Smart,* because living in a modern trailer coach combines convenience, mobility and outdoor healthfulness with practicality and efficiency... *Economical,* because one modest investment buys every facility of a well-insulated, smartly furnished three-room home ...It's a pattern more and more thousands are choosing! EVERY TRAILER COACH manufactured by a TCMA member (any one of those listed at the foot of this page) is sold with the protection of a *standard* warranty. Any one of them offers you years of comfort and service for living, for extended travel, or as a mobile vacation home.

Ask any dealer displaying the emblem below to show you warranted coaches made by TCMA members. WRITE TODAY *for free 20-page book, "Live and Play the Trailer Coach Way".*

TRAILER COACH MANUFACTURERS ASSN.
DEPT. 610, 111 W. WASHINGTON, CHICAGO 2, ILLINOIS

T. C. M. A. PROMOTES
TRAILER PARK IMPROVEMENT

"GOOD TRAILER PARKS EVERYWHERE" is the objective of an extensive and continuous TCMA program for park establishment and improvement. One phase is a nation-wide inspection-and-approval tour of trailer parks by TCMA's Parks Director, J. Lee Brown, an authority on trailer living.

TRAILER PARKS are a profitable business for individuals, business groups, communities. For advice in starting a park, address Parks Department, Trailer Coach Manufacturers Ass'n, Dept. 610, 111 W. Washington, Chicago 2, Ill.

Smart kitchens—planned and equipped for easy cooking!

BE SURE TO GET ONE OF THESE WARRANTED COACHES

ADAMS · ALMA · AMERICAN · COLUMBIA · CONTINENTAL CONWAY · DREXLER · DUO · ELCAR · GENERAL · GLIDER HOOSIER RAMBLER · HOWARD · INDIAN · IRONWOOD LA SALLE · LIBERTY · LIGHTHOUSE · LUXOR · MAIN-LINE MODERN · NATIONAL · NEW MOON · OWOSSO · PALACE PAN AMERICAN · PRAIRIE SCHOONER · STREAMLITE SCHULT · ROYCRAFT · SPORTSMAN · STEWART · TRAVELITE PLATT · TRAVELO · TROTWOOD · UNIVERSAL · VAGABOND WALCO · ZIMMER

Columbia Bicycle, 1948 ◄   *Trailer Coach Manufacturers Assn., 1947*

And the winner is...

"Lor-dy, it Sure Is Quiet!"

"'Ise quittin' announces Mandy." In an advertisement typical of the pre-civil rights era, African-Americans were commonly stereotyped as the subservient Negro. The Aunt Jemima type character speaking a pidgin Black dialect was common in the 1940s. It is a reflection of a period where minorities were routinely portrayed in a negative light. Luckily for this 1940s couple, Mandy came back to her menial job — the consolation prize being a new Servel refrigerator.

»Mann! Der ist ja wirklich verdammt leise.«

»Ich hau' ab ...« In einer für die Ära vor der Bürgerrechtsbewegung typischen Werbung erfüllten Schwarze das Klischee des dienstefrigen Negers. Dass Charaktere vom Typ Uncle Ben einen schwarzen Pidgin-Dialekt sprachen, war in den Vierzigern die Regel und das Merkmal einer Epoche, in der Minderheiten landläufig diskriminiert wurden. Zum Glück für dieses Vierziger-Paar kam Mandy in ihre untergeordnete Stellung zurück – mit dem neuen Servel-Kühlschrank als Trostpreis.

« Dieu merci, tout va bien ! »

« Y'a bon moi partir » annonce la Doudou. Dans une publicité qui illustre bien les années d'avant les droits civiques, les Noirs ont pour stéréotype le Nègre domestique. Dans ces années 40, le type Banania, avec son parler primitif, est courant. Toutes les minorités sont montrées sous leur aspect le plus négatif. Heureusement pour ce couple, la Doudou a repris son labeur ménager, avec pour lot de consolation un réfrigérateur Servel tout neuf.

«¡Gracias a Dios, qué silencio!»

«Una servidora se va», anunciaba la criada en un anuncio típico de la era previa al establecimiento de los derechos civiles, donde los negros solían aparecer estereotipados como sirvientes o esclavos. En los años cuarenta, era frecuente que los personajes negros hablaran del mismo modo que Mami, de *Lo que el viento se llevó*. Era el reflejo de una época en la que las minorías se retrataban una y otra vez desde un prisma negativo. Por fortuna para esta pareja de los años cuarenta, Mami decidía retomar sus tareas domésticas y se llevaba un premio de consolación: un silencioso frigorífico Servel.

「おお、こいつぁ本当に静かだ!」

「おら、辞めますだ。マンディはそう告げた」。公民権運動以前の典型的な広告の中で、アフリカ系アメリカ人は"卑屈なニグロ"という紋切り型の描かれかたをされている。「アントジェマイマ」風の訛りのきつい英語を喋る黒人像というのが、1940年代の一般的な見方だった。それは、少数民族が決まって否定的なとらえ方をされる時代を反映していた。この40年代のカップルの場合、幸いにもマンディはつまらない仕事に戻ってきてくれた──サーベルの冷蔵庫という残念賞と引き換えに。

Mandy's giving us another chance

since we changed to _silence_!

1 "I'se quittin'," announces **Mandy** heatedly one day last month. "Can't sleep nights on account of the rumbling of that ol' refrigerator. Then just when I'se makin' ice cream, it stops en-tirely!" "John," warns my wife, "if Mandy leaves, we're sunk. We need a new refrigerator . . . *right away!*"

2 "I know one that can't make a noise," she con-tinues. And with that she rushes me downtown to the Servel showroom. There I see a refrigerator . . . *without machinery* . . . with only a tiny gas flame doing the work. Naturally, it's always silent. And having no moving parts, there's nothing to wear.

3 **Among folks who've had experience,** Servel is win-ning more friends every year. And no wonder. Survey after survey shows that the things people wisely look for in their *second* refrigerator are permanent silence . . . lasting dependability . . . continued low oper-ating cost. And Servel Electrolux is the only automatic that offers all these big advantages.

4 "Lor-dy, it sure **is** quiet!" Mandy's happy and so are we. Servel's saving us enough on food alone to pay the installments. And we always have plenty of ice cubes. "You know," smiles Mandy the other day, "las' place I worked they had one of these gas refrigerators that was 'most ten years old. Looks like me and Servel are goin' to be with you a mighty long time!"

If you look at <u>one</u> *refrigerator, look at Servel—If you look at* <u>more</u> *than one, look at Servel to see the* <u>difference</u>

"We learned from experience that moving parts in a refrigerator can be costly. So there wasn't any question what our new refrigerator would be. We picked a Servel Electrolux and find it very economi-cal."—*Mrs. Stewart W. Talley, 1812 11th Ave., Sacramento, Cal.*

It freezes with
NO MOVING PARTS!

Stays silent...lasts longer

SERVEL
ELECTROLUX
Gas
REFRIGERATOR

FOR FARM AND COUNTRY HOMES—MODELS RUN ON BOTTLED GAS—TANK GAS—KEROSENE
Write for details to Servel, Inc., Evansville, Ind., or Servel (Canada) Ltd., 457 King St. W., Toronto, Ont.

Servel Electrolux Gas Refrigerator, 1941

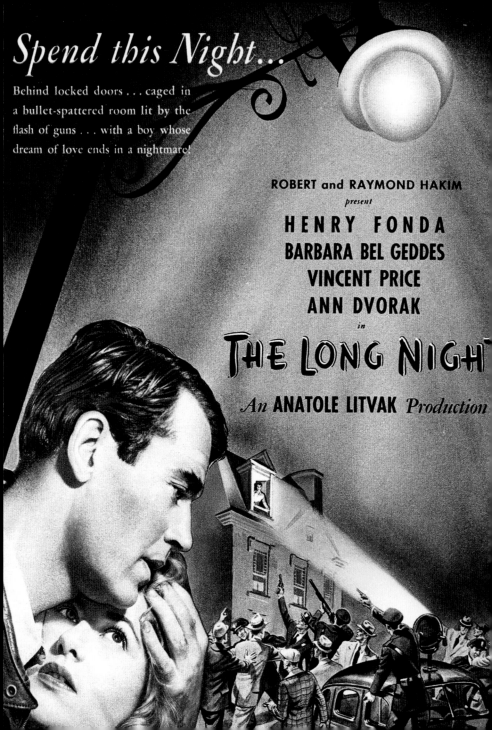

It's Terrific!

ORSON WELLES
CITIZEN KANE

THE MERCURY ACTORS

JOSEPH COTTEN · DOROTHY COMINGORE · EVERETT SLOANE · RAY COLLINS · GEORGE COULOURIS

AGNES MOOREHEAD · PAUL STEWART · RUTH WARRICK · ERSKINE SANFORD · WILLIAM ALLAND

AN RKO RADIO PICTURE

Joan of Arc, 1948 ◄◄   *The Long Night, 1947* ◄   *Citizen Kane, 1941*

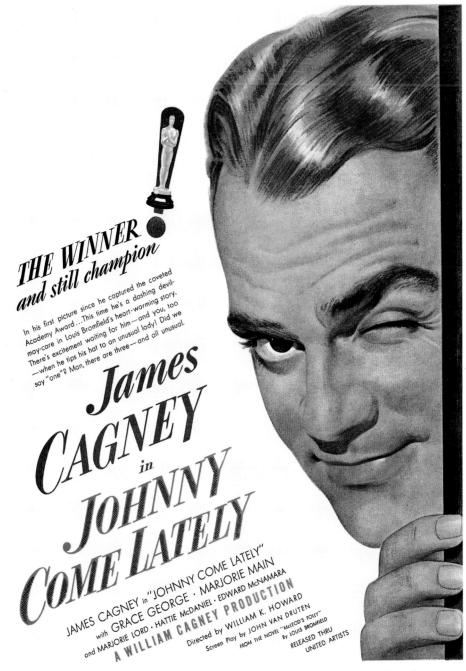

THE WINNER *and still champion*

In his first picture since he captured the coveted Academy Award...This time he's a dashing devil-may-care in Louis Bromfield's heart-warming story. There's excitement waiting for him—and you, too —when he tips his hat to an unusual lady! Did we say "one"? Man, there are three—and all unusual.

JAMES CAGNEY *in* **JOHNNY COME LATELY**

JAMES CAGNEY in "JOHNNY COME LATELY"
with GRACE GEORGE · MARJORIE MAIN
and MARJORIE LORD · HATTIE McDANIEL · EDWARD McNAMARA
A WILLIAM CAGNEY PRODUCTION
Directed by WILLIAM K. HOWARD
Screen Play by JOHN VAN DRUTEN
FROM THE NOVEL "McLEOD'S FOLLY"
By LOUIS BROMFIELD
RELEASED THRU
UNITED ARTISTS

Copacabana, 1947 ◄   *Johnny Come Lately, 1943*   ► *This Is The Army, 1943*

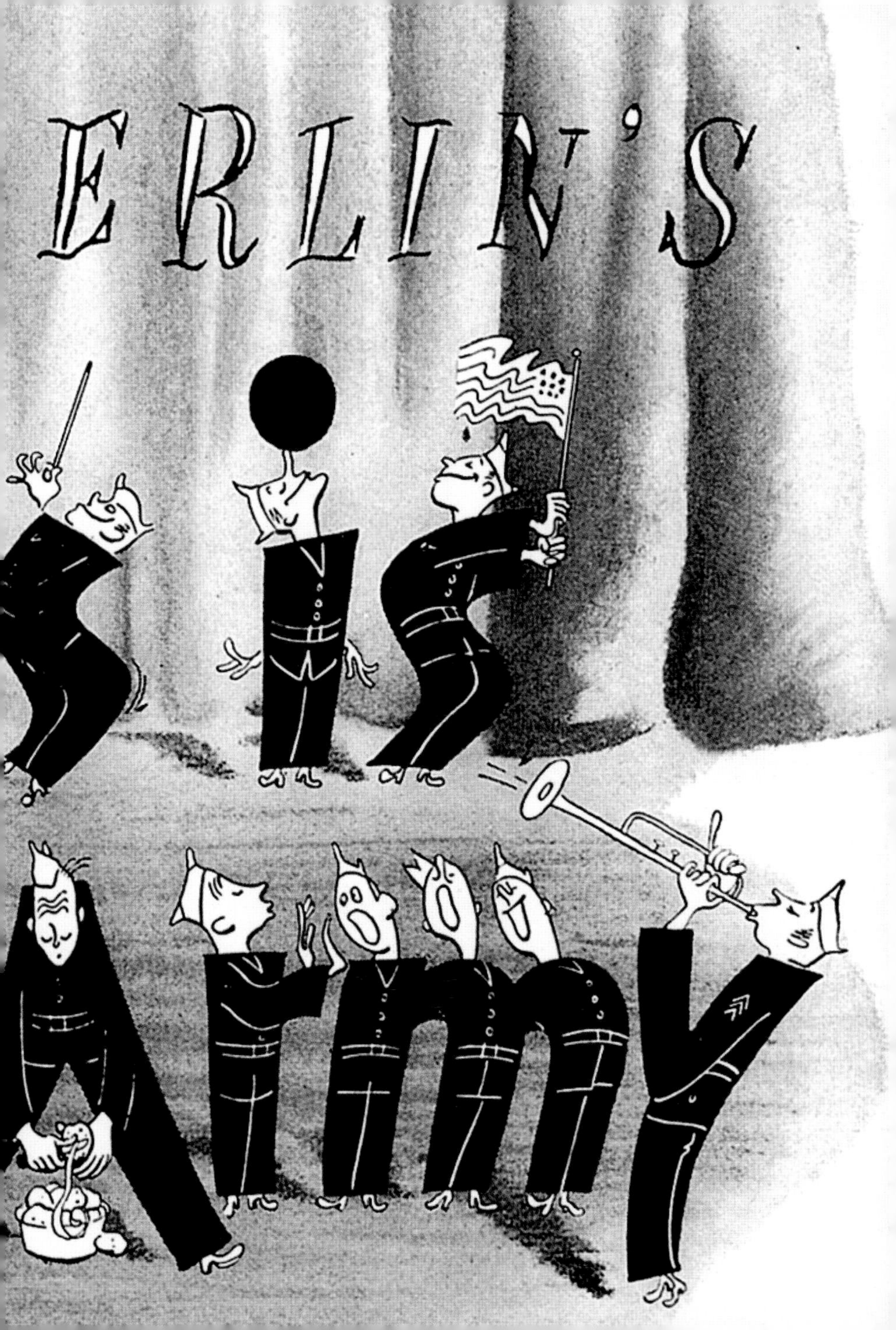
ERLIN'S

WONDERFUL! WONDERFUL! WONDERFUL!

HOW COULD IT BE ANYTHING ELSE?

LIBERTY FILMS, INC. presents

FRANK CAPRA's

WONDERFILM

"IT'S A WONDERFUL LIFE"

Tops even Capra's
three Academy Award winners:
"It Happened One Night"
"Mr. Deeds Goes to Town" and
"You Can't Take It With You!"

starring

JAMES STEWART

and DONNA REED

...as Jimmy's girl!

He couldn't
do anything
right!

He couldn't
do anything
wrong!

He couldn't
do *anything!*

with

LIONEL BARRYMORE · THOMAS MITCHELL · HENRY TRAVERS · Beulah Bondi · Ward Bond · Frank Faylen

Gloria Grahame · Produced and Directed by FRANK CAPRA · Screenplay by Frances Goodrich · Albert Hackett and Frank Capra · Additional Scenes by Jo Swerling · From a story by Philip Van Doren Stern · Released through RKO Radio Pictures

It's A Wonderful Life, 1946

► *Philco, 1946*

Beginning Wednesday,
October 16,
PHILCO
invites you to listen to

Bing Crosby !

From now on, <u>Wednesday</u> is the night to hear Bing Crosby . . .

on *"Philco Radio Time."* Yes, radio's greatest singing personality is now brought

to you exclusively by Philco, world's largest radio manufacturer. So,

to hear Bing sing, listen every Wednesday night to his brand new show

for Philco . . . at 10 o'clock in the east and 9 o'clock everywhere else, over the

ABC Network plus many additional stations throughout the nation.

PHILCO
Famous for Quality the World Over

YOU CAN'T FENCE US IN !

Wherever you go it's fun to play
WURLITZER MUSIC!

America's favorite nickel's worth of fun

Whether you're away on vacation or out for an evening in your own community, take this tuneful tip and *you'll have fun!*

Look for the Wurlitzer Sign of the Musical Note that says, "We have Wurlitzer Music."

There you can enjoy yourself and your refreshments while listening to twenty-four of the top-ranking tunes of the day. Sweet or swing, jazz or jive, rollicking polkas, catchy hill-billy ballads—they're all on the Wurlitzer, each sung or played by an artist or band that's tops in the world of entertainment.

You'll find there's nothing like good music to generate a good time. Folks are friendlier; laughter's freer—wherever you find a Wurlitzer playing. No wonder it's known as *America's Favorite Nickel's Worth of Fun.* The Rudolph Wurlitzer Company, North Tonawanda, New York.

The *Sign of the Musical Note* identifies places where you can have fun playing a Wurlitzer.

THE NAME THAT MEANS *Music* TO MILLIONS

The music of Wurlitzer pianos, accordions, electronic organs, and juke boxes is heard "'round the world." Wurlitzer is America's largest manufacturer of pianos all produced under one name.... also America's largest, best known, manufacturer of juke boxes and accordions.

And the winner is...

Here's One that's Different!

Following a long-standing entertainment tradition, this teaser ad warned audiences not to reveal the story line about a boy who wakes up one day to find his hair has turned green. Leave it to Hollywood flacks to take intriguing subject matter and trivialize it into an anonymous curiosity. This allegory about prejudice was more thought provoking than the ad campaign suggested. Quickly disappearing from theater screens, it became after-midnight TV fare.

Der da ist anders!

Mit einem alten Conférencier-Trick ermahnt diese Lockanzeige das Publikum, nichts zu verraten über die Geschichte eines Jungen, der eines Morgens aufwacht und feststellen muss, dass sein Haar grün geworden ist. Es blieb der Werbemaschinerie Hollywoods überlassen, einen eigenwilligen Stoff zur Kuriosität zu trivialisieren. Dieser allegorische Film über Vorurteile war nämlich viel provozierender gedacht, als es die Reklame zu verstehen gab. So verschwand er denn auch rasch von der Leinwand und wurde zur Nachmitternachtskost im Fernsehen.

Ca, c'est différent !

Selon une vieille tradition, cette pub allumeuse demande au public de ne pas révéler la clé de l'énigme de ce garçon qui, un jour, se réveille avec les cheveux verts. Faisons confiance aux publicitaires d'Hollywood pour s'emparer d'un sujet stimulant et le réduire à un banal objet de curiosité. Cette allégorie sur les préjugés est plus provocatrice que ne le suggère la campagne de lancement. Rapidement disparue des salles de cinéma, elle deviendra un programme télévisé réservé aux couche-tards.

Marcando diferencias

Siguiendo una vieja tradición cinematográfica, este inquietante anuncio solicitaba al público que no desvelase el argumento de la película, en la que un niño, al levantarse un día, descubre que el pelo se le ha vuelto de color verde. Los creativos de Hollywood se encargaron de convertir a este intrigante personaje en un mero objeto de feria. La película, que constituyó una alegoría sobre los prejuicios, suscitó más polémica de lo que la campaña publicitaria pretendía. *El muchacho de los cabellos verdes* no tardó en abandonar la gran pantalla para convertirse en una serie televisiva que se emitía después de medianoche.

これこそ異色

興行界の長年の伝統にのっとって、このティーザー広告は、ある日起きたら髪の毛が緑色になっていた少年の物語について人に語らぬよう、観客に対して警告を行った。興味深いテーマを特徴のない興味本位の存在におとしめることは、ハリウッドの宣伝マンの得意とするところだ。偏見を扱った寓話として、この映画の内容は広告キャンペーンが提唱するよりずっと示唆に富んだものだった。映画館からあっという間に消えてしまったこの作品は、テレビの深夜枠に定着した。

PLEASE DON'T TELL WHY HIS HAIR TURNED GREEN!

COLOR
BY
TECHNICOLOR

WHO SAID ALL MOVIES ARE ALIKE!

Here's one that's different! — so different, so unusual, so compelling, that all America soon will be talking about it! Not just the story of a boy—but the amazing human drama of a strange happening and what it did to people—to their lives, their hate, jealousy, laughter! . . . Watch for, wait for, this most unusual picture.—And when you learn its thrilling secret, *PLEASE don't tell why the boy's hair turned green!*

A **DORE SCHARY** *presentation*

THE BOY WITH GREEN HAIR

starring

PAT O'BRIEN · ROBERT RYAN · BARBARA HALE *and* **DEAN STOCKWELL** *as "The Boy"*

Produced by Stephen Ames · Directed by Joseph Losey
Screen Play by Ben Barzman and Alfred Lewis Levitt

The Boy With Green Hair, 1948

smart women everywhere

swear by *Revlon*

nail enamel 60¢
lipstick 60¢ also $1 size

For the Best Sport You Know

Sportsman
Distinctly Masculine • Decidedly Correct

TOILETRIES FOR MEN

In handsome wood-capped bottles with full-color reproductions of sports paintings by famous American artists. Shaving Lotion, Cologne, Hair Dressing, 4 oz., $1.50; 8 oz., $2.50 • Sportsman Talc 75¢, $1.00 • Shaving Bowls $1.50 and $2.50 • Sportsman Gift Packages $1.50 to $10.00

JOHN HUDSON MOORE, INC. • 663 FIFTH AVENUE • NEW YORK 22, N. Y.

Jantzen

makes the world swim

take the plunge...all you need for fun like this is a Jantzen like this to make you look wonderful, to make you feel as though you own all the earth, all the water, all the sun...as though you own the summer. The new Jantzens have this magic knitted into every stitch, dyed into every color. Girl's suit, figure-controlling knitted faille with "Lastex" yarn 9.95. Man's trunks, 100% virgin worsted wool 5.00. Other Jantzens for girls 5.95 to 11.95, for men 3.50 to 5.50.

DEEP END

TAN with JAN...for a glorious copper-tan use new Jan sun oil or Jan protective cream lotion

Jantzen Swim Suits, 1947

Tartan *lets you* Tan
never burn!

When Tartan Suntan lotion is used as directed — you can have fun in the sun with safety. Tartan, the new suntan lotion, gives you complete protection — never a blister — yet a beautiful tan. Tartan's proved and tested protection means:

1 NO PAINFUL BURN! Tartan screens out 90% of the sun's burning rays (the rays below 3130 angstrom units).

2 A GLORIOUS TAN! Tartan admits 90% of the healthful tanning rays of the sun (the rays above 3130 angstrom units).

3 IT'S STAINLESS! Tartan contains no iodine or tannic acid — keeps towels, linen, and bathing attire cleaner.

4 IT'S GREASELESS! Helps you look your best when you're on the beach. Tartan's invisible protective film is non-greasy, non-oily. No sand or dirt can cling to your skin.

* When Tartan is applied thoroughly and completely over all exposed skin areas, before and after bathing, and frequently enough to take care of removal of the preparation from the skin due to excessive perspiration.

The Suntan Lotion
Recommended above All Others
by Leading Resort Hotels.

A McKesson & Robbins Product

Tartan Suntan Lotion, 1947

▶ *Color Affiliates, 1940*

color matching...A PROBLEM

*R*emember when color matching of gloves, hat, shoes or bag to go with your new costume meant tramping - the - town . . . then wearily compromising on a "near match"?

COLOR AFFILIATES *have changed all that!*

Imagine the head of the great house of Stroock woolens . . . Koret, who makes the finest bags the world over . . . Mallinson's silk color experts . . Kislav gloves, style and color *right* for a generation . . . two top-flight shoe creators, Delman and Palter DeLiso . . . the head of the famous house of G. Howard Hodge hats . . . Elizabeth Arden . . . all getting together, pooling their resources, their talents, their capabilities . . . making available to you *now* for fall and winter wear, colors that are right from tip to toe!

That's great news...*important* news! So exciting, that leading fashion magazines write editorials about it! And *these* are the colors:

DELMAN

INDIAN SUMMER	BARK BROWN
rich, ripe russet	*mellow, harvest brown*
NIGHTFLIGHT BLUE	JUNIPER GREEN
dark autumn navy	*autumn forest green*
HUCKLEBERRY	SCARECROW GREY
frost-nipped purple	*soft, flattering grey*

Match them! Mix them! They're *planned, dyed, fashioned* for wear with each other. And to *complete* this symphony of color, wear Elizabeth Arden's new fall make-up, Cinnabar, created *for* Color Affiliates colors!

for that "custom" look, just follow Color Affiliates !

COLOR *affiliates*

G. HOWARD HODGE

KISLAV

KORET

STROOCK fabrics

PALTER DeLISO

ELIZABETH ARDEN

MALLINSON fabrics

Back to another Great outfit!

Now that it's your choice when it comes to "which outfit"—make yours Hart Schaffner & Marx. Today it's truer than ever that the Trumpeter label is a "small thing to look for, a big thing to find!"

Hart Schaffner & Marx Clothes

The Stetson is part of the man

David Niven wouldn't consider himself well dressed if he went out without his Stetson. Famous Stetson quality gives him that important "well-dressed feeling." With faultless Stetson styling, he *knows* he looks his best. See what this smartly formal *Squire* in *Sky Grey* does for David? See what it can do for you!

The Squire by STETSON in Sky Grey $15

Hart Schaffner & Marx, 1946 ◀   *Stetson Hats, 1949*

"Don't lose 'em — they're my new *Red Goose* shoes!"

SURE, Judy's proud of her new shoes — and she'll continue to be. For even after months of wear, Red Goose Shoes retain their shape and looks ... and there'll be plenty of life in them still!

You can't see all the *extra values* that make Red Goose shoes so unique ... values such as detailed workmanship, finer materials, and extra reinforce-

ments *inside*. But these and other exclusive features are there all right ... assured by the famous RED GOOSE trade-mark in every pair.

So do your purse and "point" book a good turn! Before you buy ... look for the famous RED GOOSE! It tells now, as it has for 35 years ... "these shoes are *good ... all the way through.*"

YOU CAN COUNT ON THE RED GOOSE LABEL
It means extra values inside that assure lasting fit, long wear. It means extra values inside that assure finest materials, durable good looks.
LOOK FOR IT BEFORE YOU BUY!

Red Goose **Shoes**

"HALF THE FUN OF HAVING FEET"

AND FRIEDMAN-SHELBY SHOES

FOR BOYS AND GIRLS OF ALL AGES

RED GOOSE DIVISION
International Shoe Company,
St. Louis, Mo.

Red Goose Shoes, 1944

► *Interwoven Socks, 1945*

BLACK
STANDS OUT

Naturalizer

the shoe with the
beautiful fit $**6**^{95}

$7.45
or more
Subject to O.P.A. p...

NATURALIZER DIVISION

BROWN SHOE COMPANY, ST L...

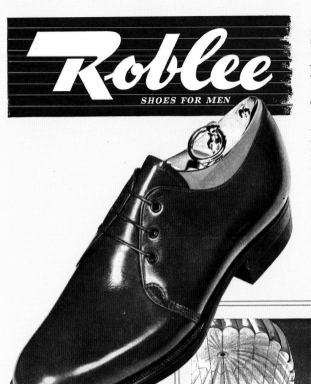

Roblee
SHOES FOR MEN

Shoes
for Men
of America

When you build a shoe for a man who may parachute out over enemy territory, or walk a destroyer's deck on a hostile ocean, you don't hesitate about putting in honest-john stitches and the best leathers you can get.

The point is, men fighting here on the Home Front also deserve "shoes they can trust."

The "civvy" shown (B979) is that kind. Hold it to your face as you would a pipe. Smell that good leather. Feel that supershine smoothness. Simple but rich and real. Long-wearing. A true Roblee*. Made by United Men's Division, BROWN SHOE COMPANY, Manufacturers, St. Louis.

$6⁰⁰ to $8⁰⁰
Some special styles slightly higher

Floats through the air with the greatest protection!

First in Sicily, hours before landing barges disgorged infantry, were our paratroopers. Landing via chute is like jumping from a fifteen-foot height. An instep "bandage" protects the arch, and toes are extra reinforced. And note wedge heel and rounded soles, so nothing catches as wearer jumps. The makers of Roblee have made literally thousands of dozens of these U. S. paratrooper boots.

*Reg. U. S. Pat. Off.

And the winner is...

In the Spirit of '42

If they couldn't don a uniform and fight the Axis, folks on the home front could at least unbuckle their belts and imagine smacking Hitler or Tojo with, what else, a Hickok belt. In the spirit of the times, almost every product was subject to wartime hysteria including this simple fashion accessory.

Im Geist von '42

Wenn sie schon keine Uniform anlegen und gegen die Achsenmächte kämpfen konnten, so sollten die Jungs an der Heimatfront doch wenigstens ihre Gürtel ablegen und sich vorstellen, wie sie Hitler und Tojo eins überziehen, und zwar – was sonst? – mit einem Hickok-Gürtel. Dem Zeitgeist jener Tage folgend, gerieten nahezu alle Produkte in den Sog der Kriegshysterie, einschließlich dieses simplen Mode-Accessoires.

L'esprit 42

S'ils ne peuvent endosser l'uniforme et combattre les forces de l'Axe, les gens peuvent du moins s'imaginer, sur le front du quotidien, flagellant Hitler ou Tojo avec rien de moins qu'une ceinture Hickok. Dans l'esprit du temps, presque tous les produits sont soumis à l'hystérie de guerre, même ce simple accessoire.

El espíritu del 42

Aquellos que no podían enfundarse un uniforme y luchar contra las potencias del Eje tenían la posibilidad de imaginarse, desde sus hogares, desabrochándose los cinturones y azotando a Hitler o Tojo con nada menos que un cinturón Hickok. En el espíritu de la época, casi todos los productos se veían afectados por la histeria de la guerra, inclusive este sencillo accesorio de moda.

1942年的な気分

たとえ軍服を身につけて日独伊枢軸と戦うことができなくとも、国内戦線の人々だって、ベルトをはずしてヒトラーや東條を打ちすえる自分の姿を思い描くこととならできるはずだ。そう、他ならぬヒコックのベルトで。当時の時代精神のなかでは、こんなシンプルなファッション小物を含めたすべてのものが戦時ヒステリーの対象となっていった。

Hickock Belts, 1943

a Jolly Good way to start the day!

this whole-hearted breakfast of wholesome whole wheat

Head over heels in luck . . . that's you . . . that's you!
For here's a breakfast can't be beat — it's Nabisco Shredded Wheat!
All the golden-good, natural flavor . . . all the nutritious full-body of the choice wheat, just steamed, shredded, baked! The one cereal that tastes good cold or hot! Every bit as good for you as cooked cereal without the bother! Be sure you're eating Nabisco Shredded Wheat — the original Niagara Falls product. It's a natural for a perfect breakfast!

One of the many fine foods baked by Nabisco National Biscuit Company

NABISCO SHREDDED WHEAT

The Original NIAGARA FALLS PRODUCT

12 LARGE BISCUITS . . . 100% WHOLE WHEAT
NATIONAL BISCUIT COMPANY

Delicious, ready to serve . . .
yet as nourishing as a hot cereal

Peanut Crunch Peanut Butter, 1946 ◄◄   Corn Soya Cereal, 1948 ◄   Shredded Wheat Cereal, 1946

AMERICA'S YOUTH NEEDN'T SUFFER
FROM LACK OF BUTTER!

It takes 10 quarts of milk to make 1 pound of golden butter. That's *concentrated* food goodness!

Buttered Spinach

Cook 3 lbs. washed spinach, 10 to 15 min., in tightly covered saucepan with an inch of boiling salted water (use ½ tsp. salt to 1 cup water). Drain, season, add ¼ cup melted butter. Top with butter. Serves 6.

Mother, be thankful you are raising your child in America! For American children are the envy of the world—and the healthiest! Dairy products have played an important part in their growth and development. And, today, their continued good health is being safeguarded by ever-increasing production of *butter* and other dairy products.

Why is butter so important? It gives your children Vitamin A the *natural* way, to help guard against colds and other infectious diseases. Butter encourages growth, is an abundant source of food energy.

Thank goodness, there's no need to deprive your children of all the delicious, healthful butter they should have. *There is no shortage of butter in America!*

Helps solve child feeding

Every mother knows

that without butter the feeding of children would be a real problem. Vegetables, cooked and served with butter, take on new glamour . . . are eaten eagerly. And butter imparts a "quality" flavor even to the "economy" foods you serve . . . makes them more appealing to your family.

Butter can't be duplicated!

Scientists have never been able to duplicate the matchless food value and flavor of butter. The formula is still Nature's priceless secret. As a spread, cooking aid, or for flavoring—butter has no equal—no counterpart. That's why the generous use of butter adds to your reputation as a good cook and a gracious hostess.

Remember, it takes ten quarts of rich, whole milk to make one pound of golden butter. That's concentrated food goodness! So make butter an important part of every meal . . . it's an investment in health!

This message is published in the interest of the health and well-being of the American people by the American Dairy Association . . . comprised of dairy farmers in the states of Illinois, Iowa, Kansas, Minnesota, Montana, North Dakota, South Dakota, Washington, and Wisconsin.

Bread and Butter Pudding

Soak 2 cups bread cubes in 1 quart hot milk, 10 min. Beat 2 eggs, add ½ cup sugar, ¼ tsp. salt. Stir in milk-crumb mixture, add ½ cup raisins; ¼ cup butter; ¼ tsp. nutmeg. Bake in buttered dish over warm water, 350° oven, 75 min. Serves 6.

copyright 1942, American Dairy Association

It's Better with Butter

Butter, 1942

► *Swift's Brookfield, 1946*

THE NEW PACK'S IN!
STOCK UP NOW

Campbell's
CONDENSED
TOMATO SOUP

from the heart of sun-ripened tomatoes
...comes America's Favorite Soup

In from the fields they come—basket on heaping basket of the world's finest and most lusciously grown from special seed, vine-ripened, picked and rushed to Campbell's Kitchens. Here, according to a matchless recipe, they are made into a smooth purée—enriched with creamery butter and lightly seasoned . . . There you have it—Campbell's Tomato Soup—"the soup most folks like best". Sometimes add milk, instead of water, for an extra-delicious cream of tomato. Your grocer has the new pack. So stock up now!

Tomato Soup—
Mmm-Good—and how!
The New Pack's in,
So stock up now!

Campbell's **TOMATO SOUP**

LOOK FOR THE RED-AND-WHITE LABEL

Campbell's Soup, 1948 ◄   *Ovaltine, 1946*   ► Welch's Juice, 1947

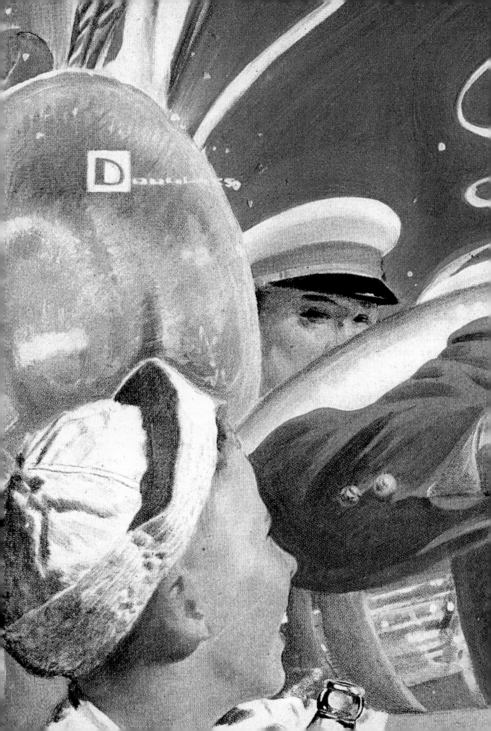

Shur-Mac Candy Bar, 1947 ◄ *Old Nick Candy Bar, 1948*

Packed with Good Taste!

● A good traveling companion is Teaberry Gum! Its cool refreshment and bracing zest brighten any trip. The distinctive flavor—that only mountain-grown teaberry can give—appeals to sophisticated taste. It's *deliciously* different! Last but not least, particular people prize the smoother, finer quality of Teaberry Gum. Get a package today.

CLARK'S TEABERRY GUM

Carry It with You Always

Clark's Gum, 1946

► Life Savers, 1943

And the winner is...

You'll Be Glad to Know it Is Reaching those Boys who Are Teaching the Japs to "Remember Pearl Harbor."
In an unthinkable headline by today's standards, racist headlines were OK in 1943 as long as they slammed Nazis or a Jap. Soldiers fortified with "Victory Vitamin C" from Florida orchards put the enemy on notice that American GIs could whip 'em, be it in the air, on land, or at sea. That is, if they had plenty of that canned grapefruit juice.

Wie beruhigend zu erfahren, dass es angekommen ist – bei den Burschen, die den Japsen die »Erinnerung an Pearl Harbor« einbläuen
Nach heutigen Maßstäben undenkbar, waren rassistische Überschriften 1943 in Ordnung, solange sie Nazis oder Japsen in der Luft zerrissen. Mit »Victory Vitamin C« von den Obstplantagen Floridas gestärkt, geben amerikanische G.I.s dem Feind zu verstehen, dass sie ihn auseinander nehmen würden, gleich ob in der Luft, an Land oder auf See. Das heißt, solange der Nachschub an Dosen mit Grapefruitsaft nicht ausging.

Vous serez heureux de savoir ce dont disposent nos garçons qui vont rappeler aux Japs le « Souvenir de Pearl Harbor ».
Dans une accroche impensable aujourd'hui, les slogans racistes sont bienvenus, vers 1943, du moment qu'ils s'en prennent aux Nazis ou aux Japonais. Les soldats requinqués à la « Vitamine C de la Victoire » née dans les vergers de Floride signifient à l'ennemi que les G.I.'s américains vont les écraser à plates coutures, dans les airs, sur mer comme sur terre. Et cela grâce au jus de pamplemousse en boîte.

La vitamina de los muchachos que enseñan a los japoneses a «no olvidar Pearl Harbor»
Aunque hoy parezca inconcebible, en 1943 los titulares racistas estaban bien vistos, siempre que atacaran a los japoneses o a los nazis. Los soldados fortalecidos con la «Vitamina C de la Victoria», procedente de los huertos de Florida, eran capaces de derribar al enemigo, fuera en el aire, en tierra o en el mar. Para ello, únicamente necesitaban proveerse de zumo de pomelo en lata.

「真珠湾の教訓」をジャップに思い知らせている兵士たちには届いていますよ。
今日の基準からはとても考えられない見出しだが、1943年当時は、それがナチスやジャップをこき下ろすものである限り、人種差別的表現も容認されていた。フロリダの果樹園直送の「勝利のビタミンC」で強化された兵士たちは、それが空だろうと、陸地や海だろうと、敵を打ち負かすところにアメリカのGIありきを知らしめる存在となった。もちろん、それはあの缶入りグレープフルーツジュースをたっぷり飲んだ場合に限られていたが。

Just ask a Jap

what it feels like to be up against men who are fortified with

"Victory Vitamin C"

You bellowed it forth to the world, Mr. Tojo—a year or so ago. *"Americans have grown soft."* Tell that to your Zero pilots today. Tell 'em if you dare! Or find a survivor from Guadalcanal—and ask him what it feels like to meet a U. S. Marine! How well every Jap knows the truth today... for he's up against men with iron wills and nerves of steel—and bodies hard as nails.

And now that we know the remarkable way that "Victory Vitamin C" helps keep those burly bodies in perfect fighting trim, we're sparing no effort to give them all the vitamin C they need. Because Florida citrus fruits are such gold mines of this vitamin, countless cans of grapefruit juice are shipped to our fighting forces. If you can't always get your canned grapefruit juice, at any rate you'll be glad to know it is reaching those boys who are teaching the Japs to "Remember Pearl Harbor"... in a way they'll never forget!

FLORIDA CITRUS COMMISSION • Lakeland, Florida

So rich are oranges and grapefruit in vitamin C, that Uncle Sam has set aside the entire supply of canned grapefruit sections, canned orange juice, blended juice and concentrates for the armed forces. Fortunately one of the juices—grapefruit juice—is so plentiful that a moderate amount is available for civilian use.

Canned Florida Grapefruit Juice

RICH IN "VICTORY VITAMIN C"

BUY WAR BONDS

Florida Grapefruit Juice, 1943

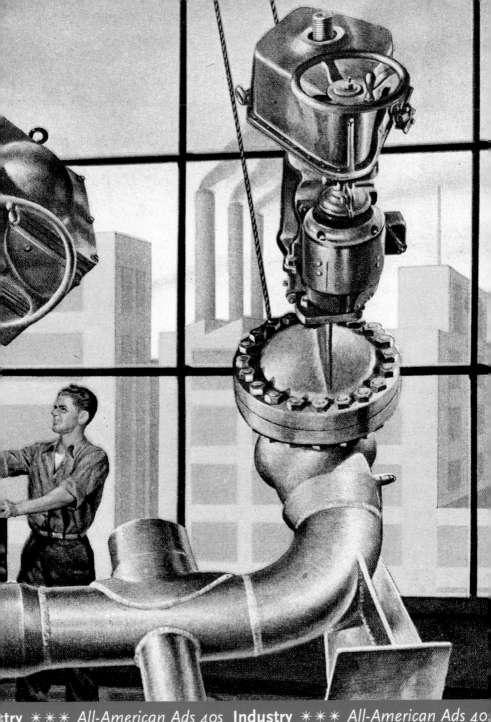

HORN...OR WHISTLE?

DIESEL OR STEAM...which type of locomotive power is better? In wartime the answer is all the more obvious. On certain hauls, the Diesel-Liner delivers the right type of power. On other hauls, the Steam-Liner is better and more economical. We can give the railroads exactly what they need in their all-out wartime effort *because we build both.* We build these locomotives with 100 years of engineering experience. And nobody can build them any better.

AMERICAN LOCOMOTIVE
DIESEL · STEAM · ELECTRIC
TANKS, GUN CARRIAGES, TURRET PARTS, MARINE DIESELS

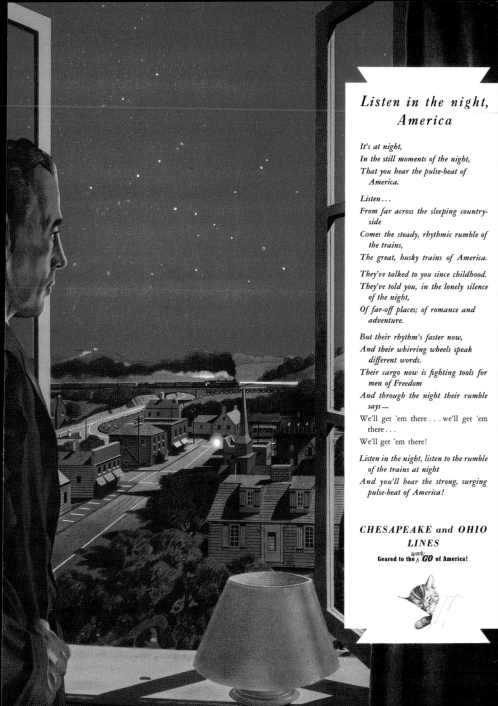

Listen in the night, America

It's at night,
In the still moments of the night,
That you hear the pulse-beat of
    America.

Listen...
From far across the sleeping country-
    side
Comes the steady, rhythmic rumble of
    the trains,
The great, husky trains of America.

They've talked to you since childhood.
They've told you, in the lonely silence
    of the night,
Of far-off places; of romance and
    adventure.

But their rhythm's faster now,
And their whirring wheels speak
    different words.
Their cargo now is fighting tools for
    men of Freedom
And through the night their rumble
    says—
We'll get 'em there ... we'll get 'em
    there ...
We'll get 'em there!

Listen in the night, listen to the rumble
    of the trains at night
And you'll hear the strong, surging
    pulse-beat of America!

CHESAPEAKE and OHIO LINES
Geared to the WAR GO of America!

Priceless protection for finer foods

Summer's harvest preserved for Winter's enjoyment

Syruping fruit cocktail with FMC equipment ... one of many FMC products designed and built for the food canning industry.

AMERICA'S high standard of eating is not only the product of its fertile acres. It stems from highly perfected methods of improving and preserving crops. Thus everyone may enjoy a wide variety of perishable foods the year 'round – in season as well as out.

Although you may never buy a product bearing the FMC trademark, every day you eat finer foods prepared by Food Machinery and Chemical Corporation's highly efficient preparation, processing and canning equipment. These contributions are fully described in an interesting booklet "Know Your FMC's", furnished on request.

FMC AGRICULTURAL EQUIPMENT

DIVERSIFIED INDUSTRIAL & AGRICULTURAL CHEMICALS

PEERLESS PUMPS & WATER SYSTEMS

FMC CANNING, FREEZING & PACKAGING EQUIPMENT

FMC PACKING HOUSE & PROCESSING EQUIPMENT

JOHN BEAN AUTOMOTIVE MAINTENANCE EQUIPMENT

 FOOD MACHINERY AND CHEMICAL
CORPORATION
EXECUTIVE OFFICES: SAN JOSE 5, CALIFORNIA

AGRICULTURAL EQUIPMENT
JOHN BEAN DIVISION
Lansing, Michigan
JOHN BEAN (WESTERN) DIVISION
San Jose, California
BOLENS PRODUCTS DIVISION
Port Washington, Wisconsin

AUTOMOTIVE SERVICE EQUIPMENT
JOHN BEAN DIVISION
Lansing, Michigan

AGRICULTURAL INSECTICIDES & FUNGICIDES
NIAGARA CHEMICAL DIV., Middleport, N.Y.
Jacksonville, Fla., Richmond, Calif.
PUMPS & WATER SYSTEMS, PEERLESS PUMP DIVISION
Los Angeles, California, Indianapolis, Indiana

INDUSTRIAL CHEMICALS
WESTVACO CHEMICAL DIVISION
New York, New York
CANNING & FREEZING EQUIPMENT
ANDERSON-BARNGROVER DIVISION
San Jose, California
SPRAGUE-SELLS DIVISION, Hoopeston, Illinois
PACKAGING EQUIPMENT, STOKES AND SMITH COMPANY
(wholly owned subsidiary) Philadelphia, Pa.

PACKING HOUSE & PROCESSING EQUIPMENT
PACKING EQUIPMENT DIVISION
Riverside, California
Harlingen, Texas
FLORIDA DIVISION
Lakeland, Florida

FIRE FIGHTING EQUIPMENT
JOHN BEAN (WESTERN) DIVISION
San Jose, California
JOHN BEAN DIVISION
Lansing, Michigan

The Pump That Puts Precision Into *Flow*

Assuring the steady delivery of coolant for machine tools, powering their feeds and lubricating their bearings are just three of the many tasks Industry is assigning to McIntyre Pumps and Fluid Motors.

McIntyre Precision... source of peak performance in so many hydraulic power, lubricating and other pressure delivery applications... is achieved by machining methods capable of holding dimensions to plus or minus .000025''... flat surfaces to one light band. What is your problem? The McIntyre Co., (formerly Zenith Associates) 100 Riverdale Avenue, Newton 58, Massachusetts.

McINTYRE PUMPS AND FLUID MOTORS

THE ULTIMATE IN PRECISION... IDENTIFIED BY THE LIGHT BAND

Small red and green lights wink on and off

... a mechanical hand silently traces different colored ink lines on a slowly turning graph ... black arrows fluctuate to right and left on a multitude of dials—recording the pulse-beat of a power plant and its delivery of electricity to the factories, farms, buildings and homes of its locale—recording the delivery of thousands of kilowatts sent out over its network of wires to keep the nation *alive*. From the unbelievably gigantic boilers whose smoke stacks reach their fingers to the sky, to the sleek streamlined turbine generators whose speed is so closely regulated as to be coordinated to match the speed of your electric clock and thus maintain accurate time, a power plant is a modern masterpiece of engineering ingenuity and skill.

In order to best serve users of electricity with all possible economy, power plant engineers bend every effort to conserve heat. Many of the nation's power plants use Union Asbestos insulations on piping, boilers and turbines throughout—they are preferred because of their high efficiency, cleanliness, ease of installation and because they're unaffected by moisture.

INSULATION FOR MARINE, RAILROAD, AVIATION AND INDUSTRIAL USE

Offices:	Plants:
CHICAGO	CICERO, ILL.
NEW YORK	BLUE ISLAND, ILL.
SAN FRANCISCO	PATERSON, N. J.

UNION ASBESTOS
MEANS PROGRESS IN INSULATION
AND RUBBER CO.

Seward

McIntyre Pumps, 1946 ◄   Union Asbestos & Rubber Company, 1944

MACK TRUCKS, INC., big name in big trucks, has manufactured transportation equipment for half a century. Shell Lubricants help speed their production.

Threading a path to the top

THE PERFORMANCE which makes "built like a Mack Truck" mean *tough and rugged*, comes from insistence on perfection in production.

One important production step at Mack is the *cutting and threading* of cylinderhead studs from high-grade, heat-treated steel. Mack engineers chose this exacting operation as a test of industrial lubricants.

Shell's nomination for the showdown performance was one of their regular cutting oils. Tests, conducted on an automatic machine, used bar steel of Brinell hardness 269-293. Results were clear and conclusive: Shell's cutting oil increased production materially.

As a result, Shell's cutting oil is now used in producing studs at Mack's New Jersey plant—also helps make relief valves, push-rod ends, oil-pump shafts, and valve-adjusting screws . . . Other Shell Industrial Lubricants serve Mack in a variety of ways. In all cases, according to Mack engineers, the experience with Shell Lubricants is one of complete satisfaction.

Yesterday's answer to a lubrication problem is seldom good enough for today. Shell's complete and progressive lubrication plan includes: study and analysis of plant and machines; engineering counsel; advice on applying lubricants; schedules and controls for each machine; periodic reports on progress. *Are you absolutely sure the machines in your plant benefit by all that's new in lubrication? Call in the Shell Lubrication Engineer.*

LEADERS IN INDUSTRY RELY ON
SHELL INDUSTRIAL LUBRICANTS

SHELL

MEET YOUR NEW NEIGHBOR...

Java stands right at the crossroads of one of the most exciting corners of the world. It is one of the string of important stepping stones to Asia and the East—steps that include the magic sounding islands of Madura, Sumatra, Borneo and the Celebes. These help make the bridge from Australia to our own Pacific outpost, the Phillipines. Today Java is Jap held. Tomorrow the Japs will be blasted out of there. Hallicrafters short wave radio equipment in the first assault wave will help do the job. The day after tomorrow Hallicrafters will help introduce Java into the widening circle of new, world neighbors. On that day, and through this medium, new knowledge, new understanding will help secure the peace we're fighting for. Hallicrafters radios, constantly refined under fire of war, will be ready for the peace with the finest short wave radio equipment available.

Here is a Hallicrafters communications receiver with an amazing range and capacity. Right now all of Hallicrafters production goes into war communications equipment. But the time will come when you can own a set like this, a set that has been tried under fire and refined and perfected to the highest degree. Keep an eye on Hallicrafters to keep you in touch with the exciting new world to come.

BUY A WAR BOND TODAY!

hallicrafters RADIO

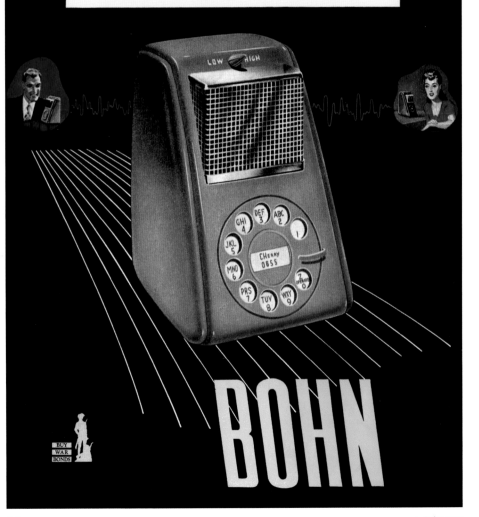

Your telephone might be like this!

Simplification is the order of the day. A telephone to which you listen and into which you talk, without having to hold a transmitter, is a future possibility. Similar improvements will be made in many other familiar products, and you will see too, a great variety of new things.

Many of these will call for wider use of the light alloys—aluminum and magnesium. Bohn engineering and research facilities will be at your disposal, in making the widest possible use in your products of the many sales and operating advantages of these light alloys.

BOHN ALUMINUM AND BRASS CORPORATION, DETROIT 26, MICHIGAN
GENERAL OFFICES—LAFAYETTE BUILDING
Designers and Fabricators — ALUMINUM ● MAGNESIUM ● BRASS ● AIRCRAFT-TYPE BEARINGS

Bohn, 1945

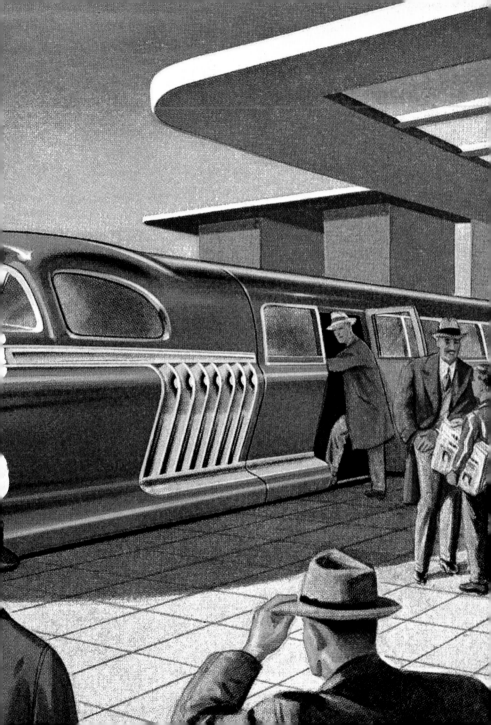

And the winner is...

One More Step in the Application of Chemistry to Better Living

Technology and industry promised a world of possibilities during the 1940s including the eradication of pesky weeds. The residual effects of spraying bothersome plants on grazing land throughout the West was never discussed or reported. The main thing was that the chemicals got the job done. What America needed was "one more step in the application of chemistry for better living."

Und wieder bringt uns die angewandte Chemie dem besseren Leben einen Schritt näher

Technologie und Industrie verhießen in den Vierzigern eine Welt der unbegrenzten Möglichkeiten, darunter auch die Ausrottung störenden Unkrauts. Die Neben- und Nachwirkungen des flächendeckenden Besprühens lästiger Pflanzen auf den Weidegründen des Westens wurden nie diskutiert oder bekannt gemacht. Hauptsache, die Chemie stimmte. Denn sie brachte die Amerikaner »dem besseren Leben einen Schritt näher«.

La chimie, toujours plus loin, pour une meilleure qualité de vie

Dans les années 40, la technologie et l'industrie promettent des progrès sans bornes, même pour l'éradication définitive des mauvaises herbes. Jamais on ne se préoccupe des effets résiduels quand on pulvérise généreusement les grandes plaines de l'Ouest. La grande crainte, pour l'heure présente, c'est que l'on puisse se désintéresser des produits chimiques. L'Amérique a encore besoin « des progrès en matière chimique, pour améliorer notre vie quotidienne ».

La química al servicio de una mayor calidad de vida

Durante los años cuarenta, la tecnología y la industria auguraban un mundo prometedor, en el que incluso se podía erradicar las malas hierbas. Para hacerlo, nada mejor que rociar los campos de pastoreo del oeste de Estados Unidos con pesticidas, de cuyos efectos secundarios no sólo no se informaba sino que se hacía caso omiso: lo importante era que los productos químicos cumplieran su función. Norteamérica necesitaba que los progresos en materia química propiciaran una mejor calidad de vida.

より良い暮らしのために、さらなる化学の応用を

1940年代、科学技術と産業が可能性に満ちた世界を約束した——厄介な雑草を根絶することも含めて。アメリカ西部中の放牧地に茂った面倒な植物に浴びせた除草剤の残留物が与えるだろう影響のことなど、論じられることも報告されることもなかった。重要なのは、化学物質がその役目を果たすことだった。なにしろアメリカが必要としていたのは「より良い暮らしのために、化学の応用をまた一歩前進させる」ことだったのだから。

"Jes' Plumb Loco!"

"Jes' plumb loco" has been a colorful phrase of our language for several generations. But, few people know its true significance. <> To the cattleman, it spells a dire economic loss—to himself and to the country at large. <> The loco weed that infests our country from the Rio Grande to Montana has been responsible for cattle, horse and sheep raisers abandoning thousands of acres of otherwise good grazing land. <> Animals that eat this tempting weed become seriously ill. Loss of muscular control usually follows, resulting ultimately in death. <> Development of chemical sprays that kill weeds has made available a low-cost, easy method to rid the cattle country of this destructive plant—just as it has made easier the eradication of weeds wherever they are. <> Dow is actively engaged in the production of these new chemicals—one more step in the application of chemistry to better living.

THE DOW CHEMICAL COMPANY, MIDLAND, MICHIGAN

New York, Boston, Philadelphia, Washington, Cleveland, Detroit, Chicago, St. Louis, Houston, San Francisco, Los Angeles, Seattle

Weed Killer
AGRICULTURAL CHEMICAL DIVISION

DOW

CHEMICALS INDISPENSABLE TO INDUSTRY AND AGRICULTURE

Dow Chemicals, 1946

SET A CHEERFUL WAR-TIME TABLE WITH...

Burlington Tablecloths

Homestead
Size 60" x 80". Four solid
gay colors with white plaid.
About $2.95.

Snack Bar
Size 54" x 54". Bold plaid
in four color combinations.
About $1.65.

Terrace
Size 54" x 54". Plaid in four
lovely color combinations.
About $1.65.

Here are gala backgrounds to set
off your nutrition-right meals ... to
add fun to calory-counting! These
sturdy, all-American, all-cotton,
woven tablecloths make formal or
casual dining an event! In vibrant,
modern colors—all Ivory-Tested
for washability. Sizes range from
bridge to dinner size. Napkins to
match. Priced for thrifty war-time
budgets. Better stores have them.

BURLINGTON MILLS CORPORATION of New York • 271 CHURCH STREET • NEW YORK, N. Y.

Armstrong Asphalt Tile, 1945 ◄ *Burlington Tablecloths, 1942* ► *Masonite Presdwoods, 1946*

Everywhere — you'll find

MASONITE PRESDWOODS

A new, proved *basic material* is used today by nearly every industry! The Masonite* Presdwoods have become a sign of quality and *efficient manufacture.*

Masonite Presdwoods are very dense, hard, smooth panels or boards—grainless and with unusual dimensional stability. They resist moisture and wear — have no tendency to warp, crack, splinter or check. Handsome in natural finish, they welcome most applied finishes.

These remarkable hardboards are splendid for speedy, economical quantity fabrication on metal or wood-working tools. They can be die-cut, drilled, punched, routed, shaped to precise dimensions, permanently bent, easily laminated.

You can add quality, durability and strength to your products with Masonite Presdwoods. Our engineers will give you detailed facts. Write Masonite Corp., Dept. S-5, 111 W. Washington St., Chicago, Ill.

Modern kitchen cabinet units, and tables, counters, cupboards, dressers, desks, and other furnishings are made by many manufacturers with Masonite* Presdwoods— for strength, durability and resistance to moisture. In kitchen units, they are used for panels, doors, drawers, work surfaces (shown above in natural finish).

★ "Masonite" is a trade-mark registered in the U. S. Pat. Office, and signifies that Masonite Corporation is the source of the product.

MASONITE BRAND PRODUCTS

PRESSED FROM EXPLODED WOOD
PRODUCTS OF THE STATE OF MISSISSIPPI

Copyright 1946, Masonite Corp.

Styled by **KROEHLER**

Its An Inspiration...So Refreshingly New!

KROEHLER
(Say KRAY LER)
Cushionized Furniture
(Trade-Mark)

CHEERING ADDITION to any home will be this new Kroehler furniture.
Its beauty is breath-taking . . . its comfort superb, because it's
Cushionized. Yet its price will be well within the modest budget.
Your Authorized Kroehler Dealer will have it available soon.

KROEHLER

*World's Largest
Furniture Manufacturer*

Kroehler Furniture, 1946   ► *Herman Miller, 1948*   ►► *Armstrong Asphalt Tile, 1947*

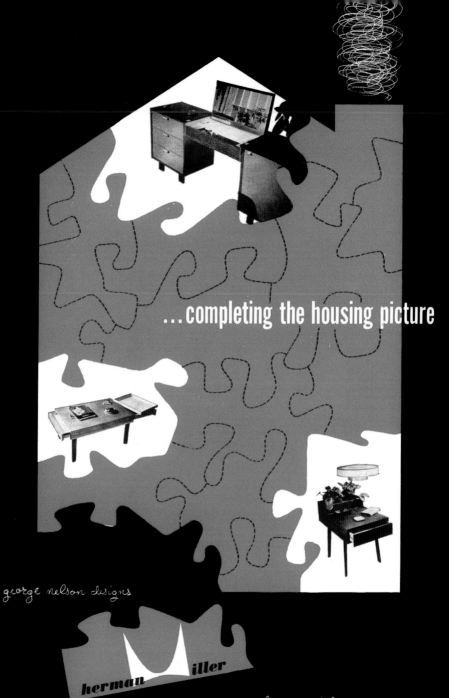

...completing the housing picture

george nelson designs

herman Miller

zeeland, michigan

Something New and Interesting
in FORMICA Patterns...

HERE are three new Formica patterns, provided in many shades and colors. They are attractive, novel and serviceable and supplement the linen patterns which were introduced by Formica some twenty years ago. The new line of modern, well harmonized, solid colors are in production and again available

The patterns and colors have all the usual Formica qualities. They do not stain with colored liquids; they are not spotted by solvents like alcohol or by mild acids or alkalies such as are present in fruit, or cleaning solutions; for horizontal surfaces they are available in the cigarette proof grade. And because of the wide range of colors and shades they will harmonize with any decorative scheme.

Reproductions of the entire range of colors are sent on request.

THE FORMICA INSULATION COMPANY
4613 Spring Grove Ave., Cincinnati 32, Ohio

FORMICA
REG. U.S. PAT. OFF.

Happy Hospital!

Why are so many older hospitals grim, colorless places? Tradition, or inertia, or whatever it was that caused this unhappy situation is fast being overcome by architectural designers who recognize the actual therapeutic value of color and beauty to the sick . . . and to those who serve the sick.

Today, architects the world over are using Formica* to prove that a cheerful material can be more sanitary and less costly to maintain than the drab, uninteresting interiors of the past.

For instance, here in the Good Samaritan in Cincinnati, Formica is on walls and window stools in training wards, corridors and nurses' dormitory rooms. Formica's smooth, tough, long-wearing surface actually repels dirt . . . what dirt might adhere to its non-porous surface wipes clean with the swish of a damp cloth.

Formica is unharmed by alcohol, mild acids, alkalies and boiling water.

See 1949 Sweet's Architectural File (section 13i, catalog 4) for more Formica information . . . and for availability of actual Formica color and pattern samples of your own selection. Copyright 1949, The Formica Co., 4635 Spring Grove Ave., Cincinnati 32, Ohio.

Beauty Bonded

FORMICA

Guaranteed by Good Housekeeping

at Home with People
at Work in Industry

*Trade Mark Reg. U. S. Pat. Off.

And the winner is...

Always Has Been, Always Will Be
Lasting beauty via lead-based paint was promised by many of the country's paint manufacturers of the 1940s. Durable and non-scaling, good old lead paint would eventually tarnish many a brain with its toxic power, affecting millions of Americans in years to come.

So war es schon immer und so soll es auch bleiben
Einen dauerhaft schönen Anstrich durch Farbe auf Bleibasis versprachen viele amerikanische Lackhersteller der Vierziger. Widerstandsfähig und nicht vergilbend, sollte sich die gute alte Bleifarbe allerdings auf so manches Hirn niederschlagen und auf Jahre hinaus Millionen von Amerikanern vergiften.

Ont été... et seront... toujours
Une beauté inaltérable, grâce à une peinture au plomb, tel est l'engagement de nombreux fabricants. Dans les années qui suivent, cette bonne vieille peinture, durable et non écaillable, va s'attaquer à de nombreux cerveaux, et ses pouvoirs toxiques vont affecter des millions d'Américains.

Por una belleza duradera
Muchos de los fabricantes de pinturas estadounidenses de los años cuarenta vendían productos con base de plomo prometiendo un resultado más lustroso y duradero. Con el tiempo, aquella pintura a base de plomo, resistente y antioxidante, y supuestamente inocua, resultó ser tóxica y provocó afecciones cerebrales a millones de estadounidenses.

いつも、そしてこれからも
含鉛ペンキが色褪せぬ美しさをお約束します、というのが1940年代、多くの塗料メーカーの決まり文句だった。耐久性があってはげにくい古きよき含鉛ペンキは、やがてその毒性によって無数のアメリカ人の脳にダメージを与え、この先何年にもわたって影響を及ぼすことになる。

**Pretty as a Picture...
staunch as a Good Friend**

... Dutch Boy stands **OUT**
because it stands **UP!**

Most folks paint their homes for attractiveness as well as for protection.

But remember, paint can't stand *out* in beauty unless it stands *up* to the ravaging attacks of heat, cold and moisture.

That's the Dutch Boy yardstick for house paint that gives lasting beauty. Always has been . . . always will be.

So when you want paint that's gleaming bright, that hugs tight, that doesn't crack and scale . . . just say "Dutch Boy." The years have proved that it's *"Good Paint's Other Name."* National Lead Company, 111 Broadway, New York 6, N. Y.

A NATIONAL LEAD COMPANY PRODUCT

BUY AND HOLD WAR BONDS

THE·FAMOUS·DUTCH·BOY · WHITE·LEAD· IN·READY·TO·USE·FORM

ONE·U·S·STANDARD·GALLON

TRADE MARK
REG·U·S·
PAT·OFF·

Dutch Boy
PURE WHITE LEAD PAINT

OUTSIDE WHITE

WAR NEEDS COME FIRST
...so if you can't get Dutch Boy
you'll know the reason why

Dutch Boy Lead Paint, 1945

Acapulco

WESTWARD, the Mediterranean's fabulous "Côte d'Azur" has moved across the world. Yachtsmen of the sophisticated set now drop anchor in the azure waters of the Mexican Riviera, with alluring Acapulco their favorite port of call. Sheer heights of volcanic mountains rise abruptly from the sparkling Pacific. Terraced palaces contrast the picturesque countryside, unchanged since the days of the Spanish Conquistadors. Your CORSAIR Cruise, aboard the finest cruise ship afloat, takes you to Old Mexico, land of intriguing color. Your days will be as full as you want to make them: Lazy hours on the white sands of Acapulco's famed beach, a dip into the invigorating rollers of the Pacific; a try at deep-sea fishing; the thrill of traditional bull fights; a round of seeing foreign sights; luxurious rest in an ultra-modern hotel; dancing in smart night spots . . . with always, the haunting romance of Latin music under a tropical moon. The CORSAIR sails direct from Long Beach, California, to Acapulco, Mexico, every 12 days. **Consult Your Travel Agent for Rates and Particulars.**

The CORSAIR! Built by the late J. Pierpont Morgan for his personal use in cruising the oceans of the world, expense was no object in her construction and fittings. When the vessel was launched, no ship as luxurious had ever been afloat. Now her interior has been completely restored, and once again the CORSAIR takes her rightful place as the finest cruise ship on any sea.

PACIFIC LINES

SKINNER BUILDING • SEATTLE 1, WASHINGTON

This is NEW MEXICO
THE LAND OF ENCHANTMENT

Yesteryear it was the land of primitive man, of conquering *Conquistadore,* of lonely prospector and hardy pioneer. Today it's a land redolent with romance and color...a land of cattle and mines and thriving towns, of timbered mountain areas and great solitudes and vast distances. Here, you'll find picturesque Indian *pueblos* where you'll thrill to the throbbing rhythm of age-old ceremonial dances...you'll long remember the lingering traces of Spanish culture and a robust Old West...you'll want to visit its many scenic and historic sites including eight National Monuments and Carlsbad Caverns National Park. Here, too, by your own choosing, your vacation can be different—restful or gay, exciting or quiet...but most important of all, you'll discover peace and beauty in this Land of Enchantment, and once you have shared it you'll never forget it!

NEW MEXICO STATE TOURIST BUREAU
Room 1201, State Capitol • Santa Fe, New Mexico
Please send free: ☐ New booklet "Land of Enchantment,"
☐ Official Highway Map, ☐ New Mexico "Recreation Map."

NAME . . . .

STREET . . . .

CITY . . . . ZONE . . . . STATE . . . .

Mail This Coupon Today AND WE'LL
SEND YOU OUR FREE BOOKLET AND MAPS, PRONTO

American Airlines, 1944 ◄◄   *Pacific Lines, 1947* ◄   *New Mexico State Tourist Bureau, 1949*

THE AIRLINES OF THE UNITED STATES
* * *

ALASKA AIRLINES, INC.

ALL AMERICAN AVIATION, INC.

AMERICAN AIRLINES, INC.

AMERICAN EXPORT AIRLINES, INC.

BRANIFF AIRWAYS, INC.

CHICAGO AND SOUTHERN AIR LINES, INC.

COLONIAL AIRLINES, INC.

CONTINENTAL AIR LINES, INC.

DELTA AIR LINES

EASTERN AIR LINES, INC.

INLAND AIR LINES, INC.

MID-CONTINENT AIRLINES, INC.

NATIONAL AIRLINES, INC.

NORTHEAST AIRLINES, INC.

NORTHWEST AIRLINES, INC.

PAN AMERICAN AIRWAYS SYSTEM

PAN AMERICAN-GRACE AIRWAYS, INC.

PENNSYLVANIA-CENTRAL AIRLINES CORP.

TRANSCONTINENTAL & WESTERN AIR, INC.

UNITED AIR LINES, INC.

WESTERN AIR LINES, INC.

Now... An Airline is the Shortest Distance Between Two Points!

A glance at the globe shows why NATS need more Martin Mars!

Look at the globe. Note the width of the Pacific. And remember, distance doesn't lend enchantment, where logistics are concerned!

How to get blood, vital supplies, or personnel across the Pacific *quickly?* That's a job for the NATS ... the Naval Air Transport Service!

NATS Swarm Over Every Ocean

Thanks to the NATS, life-giving whole blood reached the Leyte beachhead 48 hours after leaving San Francisco. Thanks to the NATS, ten *billion* letters were flown over the Pacific

alone in 1944. And thanks to the NATS, our fighting men, from Rio to Okinawa, are receiving high-priority cargoes ... ammunition, penicillin, radio parts, aircraft tires, etc., ... in ever-increasing volume.

Bright Stars in Pacific Skies

Brightest stars in Pacific skies are the NATS' new 82-ton Martin Mars cargo carriers. The original Mars in its first year flew the equivalent of nine trips around the world ... carried more than two million pounds of cargo ... was never in port more than two days for turn-around.

And the new Mars flying freighters, now joining NATS, show even higher performance.

A Promise to Tomorrow's Airlines

Martin flying boats will pay big dividends to tomorrow's overseas airline operators. Tested and proved in service with NATS, both Mars and Mariner are known quantities. Both are in full production right now ... a fact which will mean prompt delivery, at minimum costs, of postwar commercial versions. So for speed, comfort and economy ... plan to travel or ship overseas, via Martin flying boat! THE GLENN L. MARTIN COMPANY, BALTIMORE 3, MARYLAND. GLENN L. MARTIN-NEBRASKA COMPANY—OMAHA

THIS INSIGNIA IS A WELCOME SIGHT TO ALL OUR FIGHTING MEN ON EVERY FRONT.

Martin AIRCRAFT

Builders of Dependable Aircraft Since 1909

OLD FAMILIAR FRIENDS

❋ *Rommel was knocking at the gates of Alexandria when TWA crews*
first landed their war-cargoed planes on Egyptian airfields. Now,
in the air wake of such historic armadas, great Sky Chiefs wing there
from America's shores in the stretch of a day and a half.
The peace of mind you feel as you travel springs from a huge backlog
of such world-spanning experience. Twenty years of flying—more than
9,000 overocean flights—40,000,000 miles of international travel—
all recommend TWA as today's most satisfying way to see the world.
From California to Cairo, for first-class travel call on the nearest
TWA ticket office—or your travel agent.

TRANS WORLD AIRLINE

Direct one-carrier service to Newfoundland • Ireland • France • Switzerland • Italy • Greece • Egypt • Palestine
Trans-Jordan • Iraq • Saudi Arabia • Yemen • Oman • India • Ceylon • Portugal • Spain • Algeria • Tunisia • Libya

Golden hours under the sparkling Pacific sun bring a new sense of peace on the Lurline

Discover a new life...vibrant, gay, relaxed...
CRUISE TO HAWAII ON THE NEW LURLINE

Matchless days on the loveliest ship afloat. The Lurline gives you every shipboard comfort and enjoyment. Beautiful surroundings ... new friends ... deck games, swimming, sun-bathing, dancing ... star-filled nights. Food and service are superb.

Then the Islands ... like green jewels in the Pacific. Yours to explore, yours to know ... their gentle life, their flower-fragrant air, their warm beaches. Here's a vacation cruise you will never forget. Let your travel agent plan it now.

Matson Lines Offices: *New York • Chicago • San Francisco*
Los Angeles • Seattle • Portland • San Diego • Honolulu

Matson

San Francisco and Los Angeles TO HAWAII

HOLIDAY/MARCH

WO NAMES
THAT ARE AS ONE

day, those who know the Pacific know Matson.
hen they think of the Pacific, Matson comes to mind
the way to know it best. Through three generations
s has been so, as Matson vessels have developed from
ple sailing ships to palatial liners joining Mainland
d Islands with ever-increasing comfort. A fourth
neration plans still finer transport—
air and sea—giving promise that
future Matson and the Pacific
l be linked more closely than ever.

Matson
KNOWS THE PACIFIC

TSON LINES TO HAWAII AND THE SOUTH PACIFIC
SAMOA • FIJI • NEW ZEALAND • AUSTRALIA

WHEN YOU'RE FACED WITH DRIVING PROBLEMS...

Relax...

with Greyhound!

Relax **Free from traffic worries!**

Week-end and rush-hour traffic is no bother, with an expert Greyhound driver at the wheel. You arrive rested, refreshed.

Relax **You're Greyhound's Guest!**

The Greyhound station (right downtown) is a convenient headquarters, with friendly help and information quickly available. A pleasant place to start a pleasant journey!

IF there's one thing the swift pace of modern living demands, it's frequent and complete *relaxation* . . . letting down, taking it easy. And that is exactly what Greyhound offers, in generous measure . . . full relaxation from driving strain and traffic trouble—mental ease matched with physical comfort!

Check the different kinds of trips you take in a year—*vacationing, shopping in the city, week-ending with friends, commuting, traveling for business, or just sight-seeing*—and you'll find that they offer a lot more travel ease, more peace of mind, if made in a Greyhound SuperCoach. The reclining-chair comfort of the modern Greyhound bus is unequaled. But it is especially good to know that one of the world's best and safest drivers is at the wheel, competent to cope with any kind of traffic, ready to take you quickly to city or farm, across the state or the continent—even into neighboring Canada or Mexico.

The cost? Much less than driving your own car, much lower than other kinds of public transportation. *Relax with Greyhound next time you take a trip!*

Relax **Trips all planned for you!**

Greyhound ticket agents and Travel Bureaus will help plan trips, arrange popular Amazing America Tours, with hotel reservations and sight-seeing included.

Relax **Greyhound is your other car!**

When someone else in the family needs the automobile, choose Greyhound for your "second car". You will save money . . . and Greyhound's flexible schedules will fit your plans surprisingly well.

Transportation for ALL the Nation

GREYHOUND

Greyhound, 1948

ONLY BY HIGHWAY
you'll meet these 'Amazing Americans' at home!

ALONG U. S. HIGHWAY 66, one of several Greyhound routes through the heart of the Southwest, Indians still weave their beautiful rugs and blankets, hammer out unique silver jewelry, and offer bright-colored pottery made with their own hands.

Put yourself in this picture, *this Fall!*
The setting is in the vast and colorful Southwest ... an Indian rug weaver plies her skilled fingers as her ancestors have done for uncounted centuries ... the girl from the waiting bus tries on one of the rainbow-tinted blankets, and gives her own big-city version of an Apache war whoop!

Such friendly scenes are typical of travel by highway, in the sun-drenched land of the first Americans. It's an interesting fact that many Indian tribes, with their fascinating customs and costumes, can still be seen along the highways, not only in the Southwest, but in the evergreen

Northwest, among the Great Lakes, in the Midwest, in Florida, and even in New England!

Greyhound trips and "Amazing America" Tours introduce you pleasantly to just such interesting people and places in all the 48 states, and in Canada. Whatever your reason for traveling—pleasure, business, or personal—we invite you to go the way that will help you to meet the real America ... *and real Americans!*

TIMELY TIP: Early Fall, after the mid-summer rush, is the best time for travel of any kind. Transportation is less crowded, weather is milder, there is more room in hotels and resorts.

and remember...By Highway means By Greyhound!

GREYHOUND

Greyhound, 1946

Two Trains of Thought

Sometimes we think Diesel-Liners are better for a certain purpose. Sometimes we think Steam-Liners are better. We play no favorites. We have no preferences. We make no snap judgments. We study each problem separately, and come up with our answer. Sometimes it's a Diesel-Liner. Sometimes it's a Steam-Liner. Whichever it is, we build it. It will do the job it was intended to do. And it will be one of the world's finest, most modern locomotives.

AMERICAN LOCOMOTIVE

DIESEL · STEAM · ELECTRIC

A luxurious compartment on the
TWENTIETH CENTURY LIMITED

*For more than two years, this famous train on the New York
Central has been powered by a General Motors locomotive on
its daily run, 929 miles each way, between Harmon, N. Y. and
Chicago. Also powered by GM Diesels are the Central's Knick-
erbocker and Southwestern, between Harmon and St. Louis.*

"*There's something really good about this morning!*"

She feels as rested and relaxed this morning as she would had she slept in her own bed at home.

There are two reasons:

Modern trains follow modern locomotives. Since General Motors Diesel locomotives were introduced thirteen years ago, modernization of passenger equipment has made dramatic strides. But the locomotive itself deserves part of the credit. The flow of power in a GM Diesel locomotive is so smooth that you ride through the night without jerks at starting and stopping. You glide to a stop—start so smoothly that you would need to watch the landscape to know when your train starts to roll.

That is one of the many reasons why experienced travelers choose the trains with GM power up ahead.

And you can ride through the night—on a transcontinental journey—without a single change of locomotives.

And the savings in operating costs have enabled the railroads to provide extra comforts for passengers.

Fact is, the entire economy of the nation benefits as the railroads approach closer and closer to complete dieselization—the traveling public, shippers, investors and the railroads themselves.

"Better trains follow better locomotives"

ELECTRO-MOTIVE DIVISION

LA GRANGE, ILL.

GENERAL MOTORS

GM GENERAL MOTORS

DIESEL POWER

See how streamlined service steps up the tempo of travel! Only a few days ago the rail trip from Memphis, Tennessee, to Amarillo, Texas, and return, consumed 44 full hours. Now, thanks to the new *Choctaw Rocket*, that running time has been safely cut by 10 hours and 40 minutes . . . more than 24%!

Here's One of Rock Island's New Streamliners

CHOCTAW ROCKET
BUILT BY PULLMAN-STANDARD
THE WORLD'S LARGEST BUILDERS OF RAILROAD AND TRANSIT EQUIPMENT

The Diner—The hours one spends on the new streamliners pass as quickly as the miles. For radio, scenery and interesting travel companions provide diversions while the food has earned these *Rockets* an enviable reputation.

The Chair Car offers unusually wide shatter-proof windows, improved air-conditioning, insulated silence, scientific lighting, adjustable chairs soft of upholstery, with contours that invite you to relax.

WITH the commissioning of the *Choctaw Rocket* by the Rock Island Lines—an ultra-modern train offering complete travel service—the most encouraging fact in the progress toward making streamlining everywhere available has been reaffirmed. It is, to paraphrase a familiar saw, that one good train deserves another!

For ever since the historic occasion on which Pullman-Standard introduced streamlining to America and established the standards of strength, safety and comfort by which all construction of this type is measured, every subsequent train has, through its popularity, extended rather than satisfied the ever-growing demand for this modern transportation.

Fundamentally, that is why The Rock Island has been able to expand its fleet to include this new streamliner, and also why its construction was entrusted to Pullman-Standard. Because of the overwhelming preference which you, the traveling public, have displayed for these new trains, the railroads have purchased over 70%* of their new lightweight equipment from Pullman-Standard.
*When this advertisement was written

In addition to railroad passenger cars, Pullman-Standard designs and manufactures freight, subway, elevated and street cars, trackless trolleys, air-conditioning systems, chilled tread car wheels and a complete line of car repair parts.

PULLMAN-STANDARD CAR MANUFACTURING CO.—CHICAGO
Copyright 1941, by Pullman-Standard Car Manufacturing Company

Pullman Accommodations: The double bedroom offers conveniences comparable to your own home. Two full-length beds, a full-length mirror, complete private toilet facilities, a hinged table, individual controls for heating, lighting and ventilation, and plenty of storage space for clothes and luggage. Also available—economical single occupancy sections—lower and upper berths.

"Tops" IN STREAMLINERS ARE BUILT BY Pullman-Standard

Pullman-Standard, 1941

▶ Pennsylvania Railroad, 1946

And the winner is...

America Has the Opportunity to Win Undisputed Leadership in the Air
Only a few years earlier, the Hindenburg had exploded into a ball of flames in Lakehurst, New Jersey. But overly optimistic Americans held onto the dated myth that lighter-than-air travel was a distinct possibility. Despite the impending threat of war and a dubious track record, Goodyear was lauding the prospect of a three-day passage from San Francisco to Shanghai. A few months later, this type of travel would be scrapped when the Japanese bombed Pearl Harbor.

Amerika hat die Möglichkeit, grenzenlose Lufthoheit zu erlangen
Nur wenige Jahre zuvor war bei Lakehurst (New Jersey) die »Hindenburg« in einem katastrophalen Flammenmeer aufgegangen. Dennoch hielten allzu optimistische Amerikaner an dem überholten Mythos fest, der Luftverkehr mit Traggas sei eine echte Alternative. Trotz der sich ankündigenden Kriegsgefahr und trotz zweifelhafter Flugleistungen versprach Goodyear vollmundig eine Reise von San Francisco nach Schanghai in drei Tagen. Derlei Pläne wurden ein paar Monate später, als die Japaner Pearl Harbor bombardierten, über Bord geworfen.

L'Amérique, leader du transport aérien
Quelques années plus tôt, le Hindenburg explose, et la boule de feu s'écrase à Lakehurst, New Jersey. Mais cela n'entache en rien l'optimisme des Américains, pour qui voyager plus léger que l'air reste un mythe réalisable. Malgré la guerre imminente et une expérience douteuse, Goodyear propose un vol en trois jours de San Francisco à Shanghai. Quelques mois plus tard, après le bombardement de Pearl Harbor, ce rêve sera remisé au placard.

Estados Unidos, líder indiscutible del transporte aéreo
Unos años atrás, el Hindenburg había hecho explosión en Lakehurst, Nueva Jersey, convirtiéndose en una verdadera bola de fuego. Sin embargo, el incidente no afectó en absoluto al optimismo de los norteamericanos, para quienes los vuelos ultraligeros seguían siendo un sueño realizable. Haciendo frente a la inminente amenaza del estallido de la guerra y basándose en una experiencia dudosa, Goodyear propuso realizar un vuelo de tres días entre San Francisco y Shanghai. Pocos meses después, tras el bombardeo japonés de Pearl Harbor, aquel sueño se desvaneció.

アメリカが空のリーダーシップを勝ち取る好機到来
ヒンデンブルグ号がニュージャージー州レイクハーストで爆発炎上したのはそのわずか数年前のことだった。しかし、過度に楽天的なアメリカ人は、軽航空機による移動がまたとない可能性の一つであるという時代遅れの神話を疑おうとはしなかった。迫りくる戦争の恐怖と、心もとない実績にもかかわらず、グッドイヤーはサンフランシスコから上海まで3日間の旅への期待感を称揚した。その数ヵ月後、日本軍による真珠湾攻撃によって、この類いの空の旅はくず同然のものとなった。

ECONOMY — Reclining lounge-chairs in air-coach type airships will set new standards of low-cost air travel. Speed and comfort at economy levels.

ENJOYMENT — Freshly prepared meals with a choice of menu, served at roomy tables. Smooth, noiseless cruising for undisturbed dining.

PRIVACY — Cabins with ample room for dressing in addition to full-sized sleeping accommodations. No need for jackknifing.

COMFORT — Recreation, relaxation in club lounge quarters. Writing desks, card tables, library features in spacious surroundings.

Tomorrow—

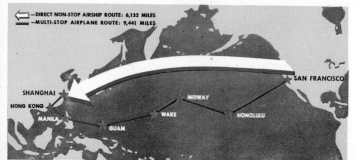

—DIRECT NON-STOP AIRSHIP ROUTE: 6,132 MILES
—MULTI-STOP AIRPLANE ROUTE: 9,441 MILES

SHANGHAI · HONG KONG · MANILA · GUAM · WAKE · MIDWAY · HONOLULU · SAN FRANCISCO

Yes, a tour of the fabled Orient from to Madras will be easily possible w limits of a two-week postwar vaca the seldom-remembered fact is: the p record for the fastest transpacific co flight has long been held, not by the but by the giant dirigible airship of the skies.

That trail-blazing flight was made ' in 1929 when a passenger-carrying spanned the 5,200 miles between Y and San Francisco in 69 hours — *the non-stop, over-water cruise ever mad type of aircraft.* And today huge 1 cubic-foot dirigibles are being bluep Goodyear Aircraft that will make longer jump direct to China — airs

hree days to the Orient!

will accommodate scores of passengers with luxury-liner comfort.

There are sound reasons why lighter-than-air transport is the most efficient and economical for all de luxe, long-distance travel. Only the airship combines relatively low fuel consumption with the high pay-load capacity essential to bring transoceanic air voyages within the means of millions of Americans.

And because of its far greater cruising range, the airship can span the vast Pacific on a great circle, "crow flight" course from America to Asia — without zig-zagging from island to island to refuel. This means a twenty per cent saving in air mileage and eliminates the weather and other potential delays unavoidable with numerous inter-island stages.

But most important of all — America alone among all the nations of the world has a sufficient supply of safe, noninflammable helium gas for airship operation. How valuable this is may be seen from the record of Goodyear's prewar fleet of non-rigid, helium-inflated airships in carrying 450,000 passengers on more than 150,000 flights without even scratching a passenger.

Thus America has the opportunity to win undisputed leadership in the one type of air transport that combines long-range, luxurious, hotel-like accommodations, high cargo capacity and low operating cost-per-ton-mile. To achieve it, calls only for that spirit of pioneering that has already made our country great in all other fields of transportation.

HITLER'S
DINING C...

STRONG MAN of "The Invisible Crew"

WHEN SIRENS SCREAM the alert and our invincible pilots of the Fighter Command "scramble" for their planes, the Strong Man of "The Invisible Crew" of Bendix stands ready to start them on their deadly mission.

At the touch of a switch, the "ECLIPSE" Aircraft Engine Starter grips and spins the engine crankshaft. Mighty motors roar into throbbing, pulsing life.

As our fighters — and bombers — take off to drive the Axis from the skies, other vital "BENDIX-ECLIPSE" Accessories take over to feed electric motors, keep radios and lights operating, lift and lower landing gear and bomb-bay doors and help prevent ice from forming on wings and whirling propellers.

And on tanks and warships, spearheading attacks on land and sea, still other members of "The Invisible Crew" move into combat with our soldiers and sailors. Skilled Bendix men and women — more than 60,000 strong — are manufacturing precision products in ever increasing volume to back up our Armed Forces — from Start to Finish!

"ECLIPSE" AVIATION DIVISION

"ECLIPSE" INERTIA AND DIRECT-CRANKING ELECTRIC STARTER

From the early 250 H.P. aircraft engines to today's giant 2,500 H.P. engines, Eclipse has met and solved complex engineering starting problems. Oldest member of "The Invisible Crew," the

"ECLIPSE" Starter combines the features of inertia and direct-cranking electric starters. An electric motor accelerates a flywheel to 16,000 R.P.M. Through reduction gearing this stored-up energy spins the crankshaft to overcome the original starting load. The electric motor continues cranking until the engine fires.

THE INVISIBLE CREW

PRECISION EQUIPMENT BY

Bendix
AVIATION CORPORATION

From coast to coast, 25 Bendix plants are speeding members of "The Invisible Crew" to world battle fronts.

COPYRIGHT 1943, BENDIX AVIATION CORPORATION

STOUT-HEARTED
shot to hell ... but heading home

IT TAKES A STOUT HEART to aim your plane and torpedo into the close-up of hell that blazes from a Jap carrier...to take it on the chin and come back.

Yes, America's Invincible Crews are writing epics in the skies over the Pacific, over Europe over Egypt and all fighting points on the globe. And with them into combat rides *The Invisible Crew* . . . a Bendix crew of precision equipment. The stout heart of that crew is the "BENDIX-SCINTILLA" Aircraft Magneto. From its battle station behind the spinning propeller and roaring engine it generates constant electrical life.

Unfaltering, these magnetos deliver over 40,000

timed sparks a minute to each engine. Supercharged, they meet combat problems in the sub-stratosphere. Bendix engineered, they deliver a sparking power that exceeds the extreme operating demands of all modern aircraft in arid deserts, over steaming swamps, and ice-bound wastelands.

The "BENDIX-SCINTILLA" Aircraft Magneto is only one member of *The Invisible Crew* performing vital functions on land, sea and in the air. The Bendix engineering mind and tens of thousands of skilled Bendix workers have put precision tools for Victory into mass production to hasten our inevitable triumph.

THE STOUT HEART OF "THE INVISIBLE CREW"

The "BENDIX-SCINTILLA" Aircraft Magneto has solved many ignition problems of all-altitude flight with new developments:

Supercharging to control sparks in the sub-stratosphere. Exclusive cam and breaker point design to insure even firing and maximum power. Corona-resistant with improved terminal and distributor point design. The "BENDIX-SCINTILLA" Ignition System incorporates a special cast-sealed ignition harness and unique high performance spark plugs. Together, the magneto, harness and plugs create a uniform, balanced system.

SCINTILLA MAGNETO DIVISION

Join America's Invincible Crew! Fly to Victory with the U. S. Army, Navy or Marine Corps. If you are between 18 and 26 apply for pilot training to your nearest Recruiting Station.

THE INVISIBLE CREW
PRECISION EQUIPMENT BY **Bendix**
AVIATION CORPORATION

From Coast to Coast, 25 Bendix Plants Are Speeding "The Invisible Crew" to World Battle Fronts

COPYRIGHT 1943, BENDIX AVIATION CORPORATION

Union Asbestos & Rubber Co., 1944 ◄◄　*Bendix Aviation Corporation, 1943* ◄　*Bendix Aviation Corporation, 1942*

BIG TRUCKS for BIG JOBS

Refueling is a big job. On our fighting fronts, it must be done in a big way. This means big trucks . . . heavy-duty trucks . . . *Autocar Trucks!* . . . For every front, Autocar provides special-purpose vehicles for our Army, our Navy, our Marine Corps, and our Air Forces. Heavy-duty equipment for heavy-duty jobs, today's Autocars herald the famous trucks that you will buy and use for rugged dependability and low-cost-per-mile performance when the war is won.

U. S. WAR BONDS
Your Big Job Today!

AUTOCAR TRUCKS for Heavy Duty

MANUFACTURED IN ARDMORE PA. • SERVICED BY FACTORY BRANCHES FROM COAST TO COAST

Autocar Trucks, 1944

North American Aviation, 1943

ARMY DAY — CROCODILES KEEP OUT!

Illustration as described by the Army Medico

Did you ever have to put a net across your bathtub — and share it with a crocodile? Sometimes, according to this medical corps captain, you have to do that for a bath — in the South Pacific Islands. Since "crocks" have finicky palates, with a marked partiality for legs, the kids put two nets across a stream and weight them down. Thereafter the "crocks" are on the outside — looking in!

You might not enjoy the bathing facilities of our boys in the service, but you'd heartily approve of their towels. For in many of their service packs are those same husky, durable Cannons you're so proud to use in your own home. . . . You know how welcome a bath and a good towel are after a trying day. You can imagine how welcome to our men after long stints of marching or combat!

They need them more than we do. That's why there are fewer towels for us. That's why, too, it's important that we take good care of those we have.

Millions of Cannon Towels

are now going to the Armed Forces. So you may find a smaller selection in the stores — fewer styles and a limited variety of colors. But the durable Cannon quality, the hardy quality that will see you through, remains the same. When the war is over, Cannon will again present the newest styles in the most charming colors.

FOR VICTORY—BUY U. S. WAR BONDS!

Cannon Towels

CANNON SHEETS   CANNON HOSIERY

HOW TO MAKE YOUR TOWELS
LAST LONGER AND STAY
"DURABLE FOR THE DURATION"

Launder before they become too soiled
Fluff-dry terry towels — never iron
If loops are snagged — cut off, never pull
Mend selvage and other breaks immediately
Buy good-quality towels — always the best economy

Cannon Towels, 1943

Because every crew must have "Victory Vitamin C"—maybe **your** canned grapefruit juice...

PT-72

is aboard Pearl Harbor's swift avengers!

Those nervy little PT Boats—daring to toss torpedoes at Tojo's towering battleships, 500 times their size! Think of it...those mighty midgets strewing a quarter-million tons of precious Jap shipping along the ocean's floor!

Just tiny plywood rascals...but not too small to carry supplies of "VICTORY VITAMIN C!" To fortify our fighting men with this priceless Victory Vitamin, countless cans of grapefruit juice are shipped to our front line forces. For Florida citrus fruits are a *gold mine* of this vitamin that's needed for strong tissues, red blood vessels and firm bone.

It's a vitamin needed daily, by every one—young and old.

If you can't get canned grapefruit juice today—better luck tomorrow. At any rate, let's be glad it's aboard those gallant PT Boats that dash from victory to victory—covered with scars and glory!

FLORIDA CITRUS COMMISSION · Lakeland, Florida

So rich are oranges and grapefruit in vitamin C, that Uncle Sam has set aside the entire supply of canned grapefruit sections, canned orange juice, blended juice and concentrates for the armed forces. Fortunately one of the juices—grapefruit juice—is so plentiful that a moderate amount is available for civilian use.

BUY WAR BONDS

Canned Florida **Grapefruit Juice**

RICH IN "VICTORY VITAMIN C"

Florida Grapefruit Juice, 1943   ▶ *Douglas Aircraft Co., 1944*

Chevrolet-built Pratt & Whitney engines power America's mightiest warplanes, including the C-82 Flying Boxcar, shown above.

CHEVROLET

America's Automotive Leader Gears All Its Resources to

THE BIGGEST TRANSPORT JOB OF ALL TIME"

on land ··· in the air ··· all around the world

BUY MORE WAR BONDS
HELP SPEED THE VICTORY

Chevrolet has produced more than 475,000 military trucks in three different types, serving our fighting men everywhere.

CHEVROLET DIVISION OF GENERAL MOTORS

Conoco, 1945 ◄ *Chevrolet, 1945*

AN ACE IN THE HOLE

Ammunition almost gone . . . smoke streaking back from a shot-up engine . . . enemy fighters poised for a knockout blow. But helpless? No! This bomber pilot has an ace in the hole. As long as his radio keeps him in touch with the ground and supporting planes, he has what it takes to talk his way out of trouble. And this he can depend on! His Belmont-made equipment has had the blessing of accuracy by every hand that touched it.

Belmont employees are giving him the best that human hands can produce. And they are turning it out in great volume—on time! Some day, these same skilled hands again will be fashioning peacetime radios for you. And just as today we pledge our fighting men our best, so too, we pledge that Belmont's peacetime products will stand unexcelled—in engineering, in design and in performance. Belmont Radio Corp., Chicago.

Belmont Radio
TELEVISION ★ ELECTRONICS

Belmont Radio, 1943

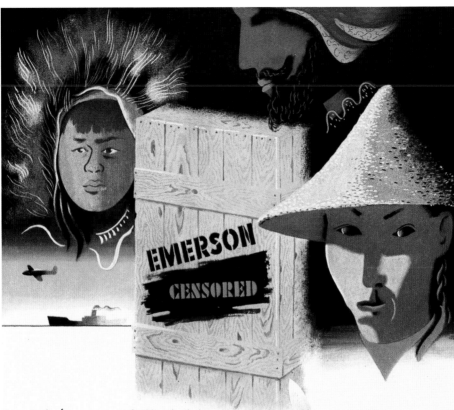

out of a proving ground wide as the world...

Out of the smoke of battle, out of the creeping convoy, out of the hurtling flight of the fighter-plane, out of the urgent drive of the war production line, there are coming scientific wonders whose war-born efficiency will one day bring great peacetime gifts to men.

Not the least of these will be new conceptions, new performances in domestic radio. You have only to know Emerson's past in this field to know Emerson's future. For in the midst of Emerson's all-out war production there are being forged today the ideas and the practices that assure a future comparable to that great pre-war time, when Emerson was the "world's largest maker of home radios"... leadership achieved through a practical genius for putting "great things in small packages".

Emerson, leader in its field, will provide even finer "great ideas in small packages" for all America to enjoy. The Emerson Electronic Radio is on the way.

In the meantime, we urge you to take good care of your present Emerson. Try to make it last until the new Emerson Electronic Radio is available. Start saving for that Emerson Electronic of tomorrow. *Buy extra war bonds and stamps today!*

Emerson ELECTRONIC RADIO

EMERSON RADIO AND PHONOGRAPH CORPORATION, NEW YORK 11, N. Y.
WORLD'S LARGEST MAKER OF HOME RADIOS

Emerson Electronic Radio, 1943

RADAR puts the
finger on our enemies!

Hiding above the clouds there's a plane. Anti-aircraft guns let loose—down crashes the enemy bomber.

How can you hit enemies you can't see—through clouds, darkness and fog? The answer is Radar—radio detecting and ranging equipment.

How Radar does it

Radar sends out a wave which searches the sky or sea. When this beam hits a plane or ship, it bounces back to the Radar. Traveling with the speed of light, the beam makes this round trip in a few thousandths of a second and tells you... *there he is!*

You keep the Radar focussed on him. It tells you his direction, distance, speed, whether he's climbing or descending. Having this information, gunners direct their fire with deadly accuracy.

★   ★   ★

Radar is the result of the work of many research groups in this country and abroad. Bell Telephone Laboratories has played an important part in its development. Western Electric today is one of the world's largest manufacturers of Radar.

Western Electric

IN PEACE...SOURCE OF SUPPLY FOR THE BELL SYSTEM.
IN WAR...ARSENAL OF COMMUNICATIONS EQUIPMENT.

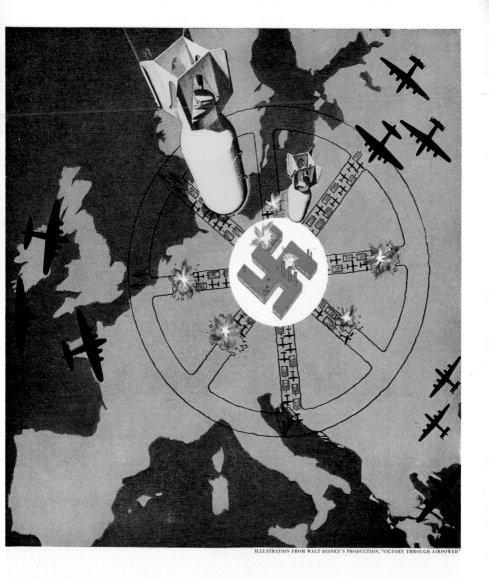

ILLUSTRATION FROM WALT DISNEY'S PRODUCTION, "VICTORY THROUGH AIRPOWER"

Blast the hub and smash the wheel!

LOOK TO *Lockheed* FOR LEADERSHIP

LOCKHEED AIRCRAFT CORPORATION · BURBANK, CALIFORNIA